Knowledge Workers
Complete Self-Assessment Gu

C000140688

The guidance in this Self-Assessment is   .....ge workers best practices and standards in business process architecture, design and quality management. The guidance is also based on the professional judgment of the individual collaborators listed in the Acknowledgments.

Notice of rights

Trademarks

Table of Contents

About The Art of Service

The Art of Service, Business Process Architects since 2000, is dedicated to helping stakeholders achieve excellence.

Defining, designing, creating, and implementing a process to solve a stakeholders challenge or meet an objective is the most valuable role… In EVERY group, company, organization and department.

Unless you're talking a one-time, single-use project, there should be a process. Whether that process is managed and implemented by humans, AI, or a combination of the two, it needs to be designed by someone with a complex enough perspective to ask the right questions.

Someone capable of asking the right questions and step back and say, 'What are we really trying to accomplish here? And is there a different way to look at it?'

With The Art of Service's Standard Requirements Self-Assessments, we empower people who can do just that — whether their title is marketer, entrepreneur, manager, salesperson, consultant, Business Process Manager, executive assistant, IT Manager, CIO etc... —they are the people who rule the future. They are people who watch the process as it happens, and ask the right questions to make the process work better.

Contact us when you need any support with this Self-Assessment and any help with templates, blue-prints and examples of standard documents you might need:

http://theartofservice.com
service@theartofservice.com

Included Resources - how to access

Included with your purchase of the book is the Knowledge

Workers Self-Assessment Spreadsheet Dashboard which contains all questions and Self-Assessment areas and auto-generates insights, graphs, and project RACI planning - all with examples to get you started right away.

How? Simply send an email to
access@theartofservice.com
with this books' title in the subject to get the
Knowledge Workers Self Assessment Tool right away.

You will receive the following contents with New and Updated specific criteria:

• The latest quick edition of the book in PDF

• The latest complete edition of the book in PDF, which criteria correspond to the criteria in...

• The Self-Assessment Excel Dashboard, and...

• Example pre-filled Self-Assessment Excel Dashboard to get familiar with results generation

• In-depth specific Checklists covering the topic

• Project management checklists and templates to assist with implementation

INCLUDES LIFETIME SELF ASSESSMENT UPDATES

Every self assessment comes with Lifetime Updates and Lifetime Free Updated Books. Lifetime Updates is an industry-first feature which allows you to receive verified self assessment updates, ensuring you always have the most accurate information at your fingertips.

Get it now- you will be glad you did - do it now, before you forget.

Send an email to **access@theartofservice.com** with this books' title in the subject to get the Knowledge Workers Self Assessment Tool right away.

Purpose of this Self-Assessment

This Self-Assessment has been developed to improve understanding of the requirements and elements of Knowledge Workers, based on best practices and standards in business process architecture, design and quality management.

It is designed to allow for a rapid Self-Assessment to determine how closely existing management practices and procedures correspond to the elements of the Self-Assessment.

The criteria of requirements and elements of Knowledge Workers have been rephrased in the format of a Self-Assessment questionnaire, with a seven-criterion scoring system, as explained in this document.

In this format, even with limited background knowledge of Knowledge Workers, a manager can quickly review existing operations to determine how they measure up to the standards. This in turn can serve as the starting point of a 'gap analysis' to identify management tools or system elements that might usefully be implemented in the organization to help improve overall performance.

How to use the Self-Assessment

On the following pages are a series of questions to identify to what extent your Knowledge Workers initiative is complete in comparison to the requirements set in standards.

To facilitate answering the questions, there is a space in front of each question to enter a score on a scale of '1' to '5'.

1 Strongly Disagree

2 Disagree

3 Neutral

4 Agree

5 Strongly Agree

Read the question and rate it with the following in front of mind:

'In my belief, the answer to this question is clearly defined'.

There are two ways in which you can choose to interpret this statement;
1. how aware are you that the answer to the question is clearly defined
2. for more in-depth analysis you can choose to gather evidence and confirm the answer to the question. This obviously will take more time, most Self-Assessment users opt for the first way to interpret the question and dig deeper later on based on the outcome of the overall Self-Assessment.

A score of '1' would mean that the answer is not clear at all, where a '5' would mean the answer is crystal clear and defined. Leave emtpy when the question is not applicable or you don't want to answer it, you can skip it without affecting your score. Write your score in the space provided.

After you have responded to all the appropriate statements in each section, compute your average score for that section, using the formula provided, and round to the nearest tenth. Then transfer to the corresponding spoke in the Knowledge Workers Scorecard on the second next page of the Self-Assessment.

Your completed Knowledge Workers Scorecard will give you a clear presentation of which Knowledge Workers areas need attention.

Knowledge Workers Scorecard Example

Example of how the finalized Scorecard can look like:

Knowledge Workers
Scorecard

Your Scores:

RECOGNIZE

SUSTAIN

DEFINE

CONTROL

MEASURE

IMPROVE

ANALYZE

BEGINNING OF THE SELF-ASSESSMENT:

CRITERION #1: RECOGNIZE

INTENT: Be aware of the need for change. Recognize that there is an unfavorable variation, problem or symptom.

In my belief, the answer to this question is clearly defined:

5 Strongly Agree

4 Agree

3 Neutral

2 Disagree

1 Strongly Disagree

1. How does it fit into your organizational needs and tasks?
<--- Score

2. Is the quality assurance team identified?
<--- Score

3. Are you dealing with any of the same issues today as yesterday? What can you do about this?

<--- Score

4. What prevents you from making the changes you know will make you a more effective knowledge workers leader?
<--- Score

5. What knowledge workers problem should be solved?
<--- Score

6. What are the timeframes required to resolve each of the issues/problems?
<--- Score

7. What is the knowledge workers problem definition? What do you need to resolve?
<--- Score

8. Are problem definition and motivation clearly presented?
<--- Score

9. What tools and technologies are needed for a custom knowledge workers project?
<--- Score

10. Do you know what you need to know about knowledge workers?
<--- Score

11. When a knowledge workers manager recognizes a problem, what options are available?
<--- Score

12. Is it clear when you think of the day ahead of you

what activities and tasks you need to complete?
<--- Score

13. What is the smallest subset of the problem you can usefully solve?
<--- Score

14. Which needs are not included or involved?
<--- Score

15. How are you going to measure success?
<--- Score

16. Are controls defined to recognize and contain problems?
<--- Score

17. Have you identified your knowledge workers key performance indicators?
<--- Score

18. What situation(s) led to this knowledge workers Self Assessment?
<--- Score

19. What knowledge workers capabilities do you need?
<--- Score

20. What are the stakeholder objectives to be achieved with knowledge workers?
<--- Score

21. Why is this needed?
<--- Score

22. Are losses recognized in a timely manner?
<--- Score

23. What vendors make products that address the knowledge workers needs?
<--- Score

24. What should be considered when identifying available resources, constraints, and deadlines?
<--- Score

25. What are the minority interests and what amount of minority interests can be recognized?
<--- Score

26. Are there any revenue recognition issues?
<--- Score

27. Who needs to know about knowledge workers?
<--- Score

28. Will knowledge workers deliverables need to be tested and, if so, by whom?
<--- Score

29. What training and capacity building actions are needed to implement proposed reforms?
<--- Score

30. What are the knowledge workers resources needed?
<--- Score

31. What else needs to be measured?
<--- Score

32. How do you identify subcontractor relationships?
<--- Score

33. What activities does the governance board need to consider?
<--- Score

34. Who are your key stakeholders who need to sign off?
<--- Score

35. What knowledge workers events should you attend?
<--- Score

36. What does knowledge workers success mean to the stakeholders?
<--- Score

37. What is the recognized need?
<--- Score

38. What is the problem or issue?
<--- Score

39. Whom do you really need or want to serve?
<--- Score

40. To what extent would your organization benefit from being recognized as a award recipient?
<--- Score

41. Are there any specific expectations or concerns about the knowledge workers team, knowledge workers itself?
<--- Score

42. What is the extent or complexity of the knowledge workers problem?
<--- Score

43. Are there recognized knowledge workers problems?
<--- Score

44. Did you miss any major knowledge workers issues?
<--- Score

45. Will it solve real problems?
<--- Score

46. Key problem solving knowledge resides with the knowledge workers, and not the manager. So, how do you adapt project management techniques to deal with this key reality?
<--- Score

47. What is the problem and/or vulnerability?
<--- Score

48. Are employees recognized or rewarded for performance that demonstrates the highest levels of integrity?
<--- Score

49. As a sponsor, customer or management, how important is it to meet goals, objectives?
<--- Score

50. How can auditing be a preventative security measure?

<--- Score

51. What creative shifts do you need to take?
<--- Score

52. What do you need to start doing?
<--- Score

53. Looking at each person individually – does every one have the qualities which are needed to work in this group?
<--- Score

54. How are the knowledge workers's objectives aligned to the group's overall stakeholder strategy?
<--- Score

55. Why the need?
<--- Score

56. What are the expected benefits of knowledge workers to the stakeholder?
<--- Score

57. What problems are you facing and how do you consider knowledge workers will circumvent those obstacles?
<--- Score

58. Will new equipment/products be required to facilitate knowledge workers delivery, for example is new software needed?
<--- Score

59. How much are sponsors, customers, partners, stakeholders involved in knowledge workers? In other

words, what are the risks, if knowledge workers does not deliver successfully?
<--- Score

60. To what extent does each concerned units management team recognize knowledge workers as an effective investment?
<--- Score

61. Do you need to avoid or amend any knowledge workers activities?
<--- Score

62. Who should resolve the knowledge workers issues?
<--- Score

63. How are training requirements identified?
<--- Score

64. Think about the people you identified for your knowledge workers project and the project responsibilities you would assign to them, what kind of training do you think they would need to perform these responsibilities effectively?
<--- Score

65. Are employees recognized for desired behaviors?
<--- Score

66. Who else hopes to benefit from it?
<--- Score

67. What do employees need in the short term?
<--- Score

68. Who needs what information?
<--- Score

69. Where is training needed?
<--- Score

70. What needs to be done?
<--- Score

71. What knowledge workers coordination do you need?
<--- Score

72. Who needs to know?
<--- Score

73. How do you recognize an knowledge workers objection?
<--- Score

74. Will a response program recognize when a crisis occurs and provide some level of response?
<--- Score

75. How do you take a forward-looking perspective in identifying knowledge workers research related to market response and models?
<--- Score

76. What are your needs in relation to knowledge workers skills, labor, equipment, and markets?
<--- Score

77. How do you assess your knowledge workers workforce capability and capacity needs, including skills, competencies, and staffing levels?

<--- Score

78. Do you have/need 24-hour access to key personnel?
<--- Score

79. Is it needed?
<--- Score

80. How many trainings, in total, are needed?
<--- Score

81. Does knowledge workers create potential expectations in other areas that need to be recognized and considered?
<--- Score

82. Would you recognize a threat from the inside?
<--- Score

83. Are there knowledge workers problems defined?
<--- Score

84. For your knowledge workers project, identify and describe the business environment, is there more than one layer to the business environment?
<--- Score

85. Can management personnel recognize the monetary benefit of knowledge workers?
<--- Score

86. Which information does the knowledge workers business case need to include?
<--- Score

87. Who needs budgets?
<--- Score

88. Which issues are too important to ignore?
<--- Score

89. How do you identify the kinds of information that you will need?
<--- Score

90. Consider your own knowledge workers project, what types of organizational problems do you think might be causing or affecting your problem, based on the work done so far?
<--- Score

91. Does the problem have ethical dimensions?
<--- Score

92. What resources or support might you need?
<--- Score

93. Is the need for organizational change recognized?
<--- Score

94. Do you need different information or graphics?
<--- Score

95. What would happen if knowledge workers weren't done?
<--- Score

96. Are there regulatory / compliance issues?
<--- Score

97. What extra resources will you need?

<--- Score

98. What needs to stay?
<--- Score

99. Where do you need to exercise leadership?
<--- Score

100. What are the clients issues and concerns?
<--- Score

101. Does your organization need more knowledge workers education?
<--- Score

Add up total points for this section:
_ _ _ _ _ = Total points for this section

Divided by: _ _ _ _ _ _ (number of statements answered) = _ _ _ _ _ _
Average score for this section

Transfer your score to the knowledge workers Index at the beginning of the Self-Assessment.

CRITERION #2: DEFINE:

INTENT: Formulate the stakeholder problem. Define the problem, needs and objectives.

In my belief, the answer to this question is clearly defined:

5 Strongly Agree

4 Agree

3 Neutral

2 Disagree

1 Strongly Disagree

1. What is a worst-case scenario for losses?
<--- Score

2. When are meeting minutes sent out? Who is on the distribution list?
<--- Score

3. Are task requirements clearly defined?
<--- Score

4. Is there a completed SIPOC representation, describing the Suppliers, Inputs, Process, Outputs, and Customers?
<--- Score

5. What are (control) requirements for knowledge workers Information?
<--- Score

6. Is there regularly 100% attendance at the team meetings? If not, have appointed substitutes attended to preserve cross-functionality and full representation?
<--- Score

7. Do you have a knowledge workers success story or case study ready to tell and share?
<--- Score

8. What would be the goal or target for a knowledge workers's improvement team?
<--- Score

9. Is data collected and displayed to better understand customer(s) critical needs and requirements.
<--- Score

10. If substitutes have been appointed, have they been briefed on the knowledge workers goals and received regular communications as to the progress to date?
<--- Score

11. Who defines (or who defined) the rules and roles?
<--- Score

12. Has a high-level 'as is' process map been completed, verified and validated?
<--- Score

13. How was the 'as is' process map developed, reviewed, verified and validated?
<--- Score

14. Do you all define knowledge workers in the same way?
<--- Score

15. What critical content must be communicated – who, what, when, where, and how?
<--- Score

16. What is out of scope?
<--- Score

17. What are the boundaries of the scope? What is in bounds and what is not? What is the start point? What is the stop point?
<--- Score

18. Who approved the knowledge workers scope?
<--- Score

19. What is the scope?
<--- Score

20. What is in scope?
<--- Score

21. How do you catch knowledge workers definition inconsistencies?

<--- Score

22. Is the current 'as is' process being followed? If not, what are the discrepancies?
<--- Score

23. What are the knowledge workers tasks and definitions?
<--- Score

24. How can the value of knowledge workers be defined?
<--- Score

25. Is there a completed, verified, and validated high-level 'as is' (not 'should be' or 'could be') stakeholder process map?
<--- Score

26. How will the knowledge workers team and the group measure complete success of knowledge workers?
<--- Score

27. Are there any constraints known that bear on the ability to perform knowledge workers work? How is the team addressing them?
<--- Score

28. Have the customer needs been translated into specific, measurable requirements? How?
<--- Score

29. What customer feedback methods were used to solicit their input?
<--- Score

30. What is the definition of success?
<--- Score

31. How do you manage scope?
<--- Score

32. Has anyone else (internal or external to the group) attempted to solve this problem or a similar one before? If so, what knowledge can be leveraged from these previous efforts?
<--- Score

33. Who are the knowledge workers improvement team members, including Management Leads and Coaches?
<--- Score

34. Is knowledge workers linked to key stakeholder goals and objectives?
<--- Score

35. Has the direction changed at all during the course of knowledge workers? If so, when did it change and why?
<--- Score

36. What information should you gather?
<--- Score

37. What are the record-keeping requirements of knowledge workers activities?
<--- Score

38. The political context: who holds power?
<--- Score

39. How is the team tracking and documenting its work?
<--- Score

40. What are the compelling stakeholder reasons for embarking on knowledge workers?
<--- Score

41. When is the estimated completion date?
<--- Score

42. How do you gather requirements?
<--- Score

43. What is the worst case scenario?
<--- Score

44. How do you hand over knowledge workers context?
<--- Score

45. When is/was the knowledge workers start date?
<--- Score

46. How would you define the culture at your organization, how susceptible is it to knowledge workers changes?
<--- Score

47. Are resources adequate for the scope?
<--- Score

48. What gets examined?
<--- Score

49. What scope do you want your strategy to cover?
<--- Score

50. How do you keep key subject matter experts in the loop?
<--- Score

51. What are the rough order estimates on cost savings/opportunities that knowledge workers brings?
<--- Score

52. How will variation in the actual durations of each activity be dealt with to ensure that the expected knowledge workers results are met?
<--- Score

53. What information do you gather?
<--- Score

54. What specifically is the problem? Where does it occur? When does it occur? What is its extent?
<--- Score

55. What knowledge or experience is required?
<--- Score

56. Are customer(s) identified and segmented according to their different needs and requirements?
<--- Score

57. Is scope creep really all bad news?
<--- Score

58. How did the knowledge workers manager receive input to the development of a knowledge workers

improvement plan and the estimated completion dates/times of each activity?
<--- Score

59. What are the core elements of the knowledge workers business case?
<--- Score

60. Is knowledge workers currently on schedule according to the plan?
<--- Score

61. How do you build the right business case?
<--- Score

62. Has everyone on the team, including the team leaders, been properly trained?
<--- Score

63. Do the problem and goal statements meet the SMART criteria (specific, measurable, attainable, relevant, and time-bound)?
<--- Score

64. Has the knowledge workers work been fairly and/ or equitably divided and delegated among team members who are qualified and capable to perform the work? Has everyone contributed?
<--- Score

65. How do you gather the stories?
<--- Score

66. Is there any additional knowledge workers definition of success?
<--- Score

67. Are approval levels defined for contracts and supplements to contracts?
<--- Score

68. Are there different segments of customers?
<--- Score

69. Is there a clear knowledge workers case definition?
<--- Score

70. What key stakeholder process output measure(s) does knowledge workers leverage and how?
<--- Score

71. Do you have organizational privacy requirements?
<--- Score

72. Has a team charter been developed and communicated?
<--- Score

73. What happens if knowledge workers's scope changes?
<--- Score

74. Are accountability and ownership for knowledge workers clearly defined?
<--- Score

75. Is the knowledge workers scope manageable?
<--- Score

76. Has the improvement team collected the 'voice of the customer' (obtained feedback – qualitative and quantitative)?

<--- Score

77. Does the team have regular meetings?
<--- Score

78. Who is gathering information?
<--- Score

79. What is the context?
<--- Score

80. Is the improvement team aware of the different versions of a process: what they think it is vs. what it actually is vs. what it should be vs. what it could be?
<--- Score

81. What is out-of-scope initially?
<--- Score

82. Are the knowledge workers requirements testable?
<--- Score

83. What defines best in class?
<--- Score

84. How do you manage changes in knowledge workers requirements?
<--- Score

85. In what way can you redefine the criteria of choice clients have in your category in your favor?
<--- Score

86. Are audit criteria, scope, frequency and methods defined?

<--- Score

87. What baselines are required to be defined and managed?
<--- Score

88. How are consistent knowledge workers definitions important?
<--- Score

89. Is there a critical path to deliver knowledge workers results?
<--- Score

90. What intelligence can you gather?
<--- Score

91. Is the team adequately staffed with the desired cross-functionality? If not, what additional resources are available to the team?
<--- Score

92. Are all requirements met?
<--- Score

93. Are roles and responsibilities formally defined?
<--- Score

94. What constraints exist that might impact the team?
<--- Score

95. What sort of initial information to gather?
<--- Score

96. What is the scope of the knowledge workers

effort?
<--- Score

97. Is the knowledge workers scope complete and appropriately sized?
<--- Score

98. Have all basic functions of knowledge workers been defined?
<--- Score

99. Are required metrics defined, what are they?
<--- Score

100. How and when will the baselines be defined?
<--- Score

101. Have all of the relationships been defined properly?
<--- Score

102. Does the scope remain the same?
<--- Score

103. How do you think the partners involved in knowledge workers would have defined success?
<--- Score

104. Has a knowledge workers requirement not been met?
<--- Score

105. How do you manage unclear knowledge workers requirements?
<--- Score

106. What scope to assess?
<--- Score

107. Are different versions of process maps needed to account for the different types of inputs?
<--- Score

108. How would you define knowledge workers leadership?
<--- Score

109. What knowledge workers services do you require?
<--- Score

110. Who is gathering knowledge workers information?
<--- Score

111. What is the scope of the knowledge workers work?
<--- Score

112. Are the knowledge workers requirements complete?
<--- Score

113. Is there a knowledge workers management charter, including stakeholder case, problem and goal statements, scope, milestones, roles and responsibilities, communication plan?
<--- Score

114. What sources do you use to gather information for a knowledge workers study?
<--- Score

115. Is special knowledge workers user knowledge required?
<--- Score

116. Has your scope been defined?
<--- Score

117. How does the knowledge workers manager ensure against scope creep?
<--- Score

118. Is the work to date meeting requirements?
<--- Score

119. What are the tasks and definitions?
<--- Score

120. What is in the scope and what is not in scope?
<--- Score

121. What are the requirements for audit information?
<--- Score

122. Is the scope of knowledge workers defined?
<--- Score

123. What are the Roles and Responsibilities for each team member and its leadership? Where is this documented?
<--- Score

124. Has/have the customer(s) been identified?
<--- Score

125. How often are the team meetings?

<--- Score

126. What is the scope of knowledge workers?
<--- Score

127. Has a project plan, Gantt chart, or similar been developed/completed?
<--- Score

128. What are the dynamics of the communication plan?
<--- Score

129. Will a knowledge workers production readiness review be required?
<--- Score

130. Why are you doing knowledge workers and what is the scope?
<--- Score

131. Have specific policy objectives been defined?
<--- Score

132. How have you defined all knowledge workers requirements first?
<--- Score

133. How do you gather knowledge workers requirements?
<--- Score

Add up total points for this section:
_ _ _ _ _ = Total points for this section

Divided by: _ _ _ _ _ _ (number of

statements answered) = _____
Average score for this section

Transfer your score to the knowledge
workers Index at the beginning of the
Self-Assessment.

CRITERION #3: MEASURE:

INTENT: Gather the correct data. Measure the current performance and evolution of the situation.

In my belief, the answer to this question is clearly defined:

5 Strongly Agree

4 Agree

3 Neutral

2 Disagree

1 Strongly Disagree

1. What would be a real cause for concern?
<--- Score

2. Do you verify that corrective actions were taken?
<--- Score

3. How will your organization measure success?
<--- Score

4. Why a knowledge workers focus?
<--- Score

5. Is the cost worth the knowledge workers effort ?
<--- Score

6. Are there competing knowledge workers priorities?
<--- Score

7. Have you included everything in your knowledge workers cost models?
<--- Score

8. What is the total cost related to deploying knowledge workers, including any consulting or professional services?
<--- Score

9. What are your customers expectations and measures?
<--- Score

10. What does verifying compliance entail?
<--- Score

11. What would it cost to replace your technology?
<--- Score

12. Are there measurements based on task performance?
<--- Score

13. How do you verify and develop ideas and innovations?
<--- Score

14. What are the uncertainties surrounding estimates of impact?
<--- Score

15. Are supply costs steady or fluctuating?
<--- Score

16. How do you verify the knowledge workers requirements quality?
<--- Score

17. How sensitive must the knowledge workers strategy be to cost?
<--- Score

18. Are you aware of what could cause a problem?
<--- Score

19. How do you control the overall costs of your work processes?
<--- Score

20. How do you measure lifecycle phases?
<--- Score

21. Where is the cost?
<--- Score

22. How do you verify knowledge workers completeness and accuracy?
<--- Score

23. What causes investor action?
<--- Score

24. Where is it measured?

<--- Score

25. What could cause delays in the schedule?
<--- Score

26. Who should receive measurement reports?
<--- Score

27. How do you measure variability?
<--- Score

28. Are you able to realize any cost savings?
<--- Score

29. Are indirect costs charged to the knowledge workers program?
<--- Score

30. How will you measure success?
<--- Score

31. How are you verifying it?
<--- Score

32. What are the knowledge workers key cost drivers?
<--- Score

33. How is performance measured?
<--- Score

34. How do you quantify and qualify impacts?
<--- Score

35. How frequently do you track knowledge workers measures?
<--- Score

36. What are the strategic priorities for this year?
<--- Score

37. What do people want to verify?
<--- Score

38. What are your operating costs?
<--- Score

39. What could cause you to change course?
<--- Score

40. How do your measurements capture actionable knowledge workers information for use in exceeding your customers expectations and securing your customers engagement?
<--- Score

41. What are allowable costs?
<--- Score

42. Why do the measurements/indicators matter?
<--- Score

43. How will effects be measured?
<--- Score

44. What evidence is there and what is measured?
<--- Score

45. How much does it cost?
<--- Score

46. How do you verify and validate the knowledge workers data?

<--- Score

47. What happens if cost savings do not materialize?
<--- Score

48. Do the benefits outweigh the costs?
<--- Score

49. When should you bother with diagrams?
<--- Score

50. Are missed knowledge workers opportunities costing your organization money?
<--- Score

51. What disadvantage does this cause for the user?
<--- Score

52. What measurements are possible, practicable and meaningful?
<--- Score

53. Are actual costs in line with budgeted costs?
<--- Score

54. What methods are feasible and acceptable to estimate the impact of reforms?
<--- Score

55. Which knowledge workers impacts are significant?
<--- Score

56. Are knowledge workers vulnerabilities categorized and prioritized?
<--- Score

57. What is measured? Why?
<--- Score

58. What are the current costs of the knowledge workers process?
<--- Score

59. What is the root cause(s) of the problem?
<--- Score

60. What can be used to verify compliance?
<--- Score

61. What are the costs of delaying knowledge workers action?
<--- Score

62. Is it possible to estimate the impact of unanticipated complexity such as wrong or failed assumptions, feedback, etcetera on proposed reforms?
<--- Score

63. What tests verify requirements?
<--- Score

64. What are the costs of reform?
<--- Score

65. Is the solution cost-effective?
<--- Score

66. What are hidden knowledge workers quality costs?
<--- Score

67. Do you effectively measure and reward individual

and team performance?
<--- Score

68. What causes extra work or rework?
<--- Score

69. Are the knowledge workers benefits worth its costs?
<--- Score

70. Does the knowledge workers task fit the client's priorities?
<--- Score

71. What users will be impacted?
<--- Score

72. How will measures be used to manage and adapt?
<--- Score

73. Who is involved in verifying compliance?
<--- Score

74. What potential environmental factors impact the knowledge workers effort?
<--- Score

75. Does management have the right priorities among projects?
<--- Score

76. Are you taking your company in the direction of better and revenue or cheaper and cost?
<--- Score

77. How is progress measured?

<--- Score

78. Did you tackle the cause or the symptom?
<--- Score

79. How frequently do you verify your knowledge workers strategy?
<--- Score

80. Is there an opportunity to verify requirements?
<--- Score

81. Have you made assumptions about the shape of the future, particularly its impact on your customers and competitors?
<--- Score

82. How can you measure the performance?
<--- Score

83. What are your key knowledge workers organizational performance measures, including key short and longer-term financial measures?
<--- Score

84. Have design-to-cost goals been established?
<--- Score

85. Do you have any cost knowledge workers limitation requirements?
<--- Score

86. What are the types and number of measures to use?
<--- Score

87. Do you have an issue in getting priority?
<--- Score

88. Do you aggressively reward and promote the people who have the biggest impact on creating excellent knowledge workers services/products?
<--- Score

89. When a disaster occurs, who gets priority?
<--- Score

90. What causes innovation to fail or succeed in your organization?
<--- Score

91. When are costs are incurred?
<--- Score

92. How do you aggregate measures across priorities?
<--- Score

93. The approach of traditional knowledge workers works for detail complexity but is focused on a systematic approach rather than an understanding of the nature of systems themselves, what approach will permit your organization to deal with the kind of unpredictable emergent behaviors that dynamic complexity can introduce?
<--- Score

94. What are the costs and benefits?
<--- Score

95. How will costs be allocated?
<--- Score

96. What is the total fixed cost?
<--- Score

97. Will knowledge workers have an impact on current business continuity, disaster recovery processes and/or infrastructure?
<--- Score

98. Where can you go to verify the info?
<--- Score

99. What harm might be caused?
<--- Score

100. What does your operating model cost?
<--- Score

101. What is your decision requirements diagram?
<--- Score

102. How can a knowledge workers test verify your ideas or assumptions?
<--- Score

103. What does losing customers cost your organization?
<--- Score

104. What are the operational costs after knowledge workers deployment?
<--- Score

105. How will success or failure be measured?
<--- Score

106. Are the units of measure consistent?

<--- Score

107. How can you reduce the costs of obtaining inputs?
<--- Score

108. How do you measure success?
<--- Score

109. What is the cost of rework?
<--- Score

110. At what cost?
<--- Score

111. Are there any easy-to-implement alternatives to knowledge workers? Sometimes other solutions are available that do not require the cost implications of a full-blown project?
<--- Score

112. What relevant entities could be measured?
<--- Score

113. What are the estimated costs of proposed changes?
<--- Score

114. What drives O&M cost?
<--- Score

115. How are costs allocated?
<--- Score

116. Was a business case (cost/benefit) developed?
<--- Score

117. What are you verifying?
<--- Score

118. Among the knowledge workers product and service cost to be estimated, which is considered hardest to estimate?
<--- Score

119. Who pays the cost?
<--- Score

120. What is the knowledge workers business impact?
<--- Score

121. How can you reduce costs?
<--- Score

122. Are the measurements objective?
<--- Score

123. What is the cause of any knowledge workers gaps?
<--- Score

124. What does a Test Case verify?
<--- Score

125. How are measurements made?
<--- Score

126. How long to keep data and how to manage retention costs?
<--- Score

127. How is the value delivered by knowledge workers

being measured?
<--- Score

128. How do you verify performance?
<--- Score

129. What is an unallowable cost?
<--- Score

130. How to cause the change?
<--- Score

131. What measurements are being captured?
<--- Score

132. How do you verify if knowledge workers is built right?
<--- Score

133. Does a knowledge workers quantification method exist?
<--- Score

134. How do you measure efficient delivery of knowledge workers services?
<--- Score

135. What are your primary costs, revenues, assets?
<--- Score

136. What are the knowledge workers investment costs?
<--- Score

137. How do you verify the authenticity of the data and information used?

<--- Score

138. Why do you expend time and effort to implement measurement, for whom?
<--- Score

139. Which measures and indicators matter?
<--- Score

140. How will you measure your knowledge workers effectiveness?
<--- Score

Add up total points for this section:
_ _ _ _ _ = Total points for this section

Divided by: _ _ _ _ _ _ (number of statements answered) = _ _ _ _ _ _
Average score for this section

Transfer your score to the knowledge workers Index at the beginning of the Self-Assessment.

CRITERION #4: ANALYZE:

INTENT: Analyze causes, assumptions and hypotheses.

In my belief, the answer to this question is clearly defined:

5 Strongly Agree

4 Agree

3 Neutral

2 Disagree

1 Strongly Disagree

1. Do your employees have the opportunity to do what they do best everyday?
<--- Score

2. Do your contracts/agreements contain data security obligations?
<--- Score

3. Is the final output clearly identified?
<--- Score

4. Are knowledge workers changes recognized early enough to be approved through the regular process?
<--- Score

5. How is the data gathered?
<--- Score

6. How often will data be collected for measures?
<--- Score

7. How is the way you as the leader think and process information affecting your organizational culture?
<--- Score

8. What will drive knowledge workers change?
<--- Score

9. What resources go in to get the desired output?
<--- Score

10. What qualifications are needed?
<--- Score

11. Should you invest in industry-recognized qualifications?
<--- Score

12. Was a detailed process map created to amplify critical steps of the 'as is' stakeholder process?
<--- Score

13. How will corresponding data be collected?
<--- Score

14. Were there any improvement opportunities

identified from the process analysis?
<--- Score

15. A compounding model resolution with available relevant data can often provide insight towards a solution methodology; which knowledge workers models, tools and techniques are necessary?
<--- Score

16. Is the knowledge workers process severely broken such that a re-design is necessary?
<--- Score

17. What qualifies as competition?
<--- Score

18. What process improvements will be needed?
<--- Score

19. Who will gather what data?
<--- Score

20. Is the suppliers process defined and controlled?
<--- Score

21. Was a cause-and-effect diagram used to explore the different types of causes (or sources of variation)?
<--- Score

22. What successful thing are you doing today that may be blinding you to new growth opportunities?
<--- Score

23. How do you identify specific knowledge workers investment opportunities and emerging trends?
<--- Score

24. Where can you get qualified talent today?
<--- Score

25. Think about some of the processes you undertake within your organization, which do you own?
<--- Score

26. When should a process be art not science?
<--- Score

27. Are your outputs consistent?
<--- Score

28. Is there an established change management process?
<--- Score

29. Who will facilitate the team and process?
<--- Score

30. Where is knowledge workers data gathered?
<--- Score

31. How is the knowledge workers Value Stream Mapping managed?
<--- Score

32. What is your organizations system for selecting qualified vendors?
<--- Score

33. Is the gap/opportunity displayed and communicated in financial terms?
<--- Score

34. What are the processes for audit reporting and management?
<--- Score

35. What are your knowledge workers processes?
<--- Score

36. Where is the data coming from to measure compliance?
<--- Score

37. What is the output?
<--- Score

38. What data is gathered?
<--- Score

39. How do you use knowledge workers data and information to support organizational decision making and innovation?
<--- Score

40. Do your leaders quickly bounce back from setbacks?
<--- Score

41. Who is involved in the management review process?
<--- Score

42. How are outputs preserved and protected?
<--- Score

43. What systems/processes must you excel at?
<--- Score

44. What output to create?
<--- Score

45. Who qualifies to gain access to data?
<--- Score

46. What qualifications do knowledge workers leaders need?
<--- Score

47. What knowledge workers data should be collected?
<--- Score

48. What are your current levels and trends in key measures or indicators of knowledge workers product and process performance that are important to and directly serve your customers? How do these results compare with the performance of your competitors and other organizations with similar offerings?
<--- Score

49. How do your work systems and key work processes relate to and capitalize on your core competencies?
<--- Score

50. What were the financial benefits resulting from any 'ground fruit or low-hanging fruit' (quick fixes)?
<--- Score

51. How many input/output points does it require?
<--- Score

52. What are your best practices for minimizing knowledge workers project risk, while demonstrating

incremental value and quick wins throughout the knowledge workers project lifecycle?
<--- Score

53. What are the knowledge workers business drivers?
<--- Score

54. Have the problem and goal statements been updated to reflect the additional knowledge gained from the analyze phase?
<--- Score

55. Do you have the authority to produce the output?
<--- Score

56. Were Pareto charts (or similar) used to portray the 'heavy hitters' (or key sources of variation)?
<--- Score

57. What is the knowledge workers Driver?
<--- Score

58. How does the organization define, manage, and improve its knowledge workers processes?
<--- Score

59. What data do you need to collect?
<--- Score

60. Were any designed experiments used to generate additional insight into the data analysis?
<--- Score

61. How difficult is it to qualify what knowledge workers ROI is?
<--- Score

62. Identify an operational issue in your organization, for example, could a particular task be done more quickly or more efficiently by knowledge workers?
<--- Score

63. Is there any way to speed up the process?
<--- Score

64. Have you defined which data is gathered how?
<--- Score

65. What tools were used to narrow the list of possible causes?
<--- Score

66. Has an output goal been set?
<--- Score

67. What are your outputs?
<--- Score

68. Are all staff in core knowledge workers subjects Highly Qualified?
<--- Score

69. What is the cost of poor quality as supported by the team's analysis?
<--- Score

70. Do staff qualifications match your project?
<--- Score

71. Do quality systems drive continuous improvement?
<--- Score

72. How do you measure the operational performance of your key work systems and processes, including productivity, cycle time, and other appropriate measures of process effectiveness, efficiency, and innovation?
<--- Score

73. What did the team gain from developing a sub-process map?
<--- Score

74. What is the complexity of the output produced?
<--- Score

75. How was the detailed process map generated, verified, and validated?
<--- Score

76. Is data and process analysis, root cause analysis and quantifying the gap/opportunity in place?
<--- Score

77. What knowledge workers data do you gather or use now?
<--- Score

78. What are the necessary qualifications?
<--- Score

79. What are evaluation criteria for the output?
<--- Score

80. What is your organizations process which leads to recognition of value generation?
<--- Score

81. Do you, as a leader, bounce back quickly from setbacks?
<--- Score

82. What are the knowledge workers design outputs?
<--- Score

83. An organizationally feasible system request is one that considers the mission, goals and objectives of the organization, key questions are: is the knowledge workers solution request practical and will it solve a problem or take advantage of an opportunity to achieve company goals?
<--- Score

84. What do you need to qualify?
<--- Score

85. Is there a strict change management process?
<--- Score

86. What kind of crime could a potential new hire have committed that would not only not disqualify him/her from being hired by your organization, but would actually indicate that he/she might be a particularly good fit?
<--- Score

87. Record-keeping requirements flow from the records needed as inputs, outputs, controls and for transformation of a knowledge workers process, are the records needed as inputs to the knowledge workers process available?
<--- Score

88. How is knowledge workers data gathered?
<--- Score

89. What qualifications and skills do you need?
<--- Score

90. What do you teach knowledge workers about data?
<--- Score

91. What were the crucial 'moments of truth' on the process map?
<--- Score

92. What are the best opportunities for value improvement?
<--- Score

93. What does the data say about the performance of the stakeholder process?
<--- Score

94. What are the disruptive knowledge workers technologies that enable your organization to radically change your business processes?
<--- Score

95. Is the performance gap determined?
<--- Score

96. Are you missing knowledge workers opportunities?
<--- Score

97. Is the required knowledge workers data gathered?
<--- Score

98. Think about the functions involved in your knowledge workers project, what processes flow from these functions?
<--- Score

99. What knowledge workers metrics are outputs of the process?
<--- Score

100. What other jobs or tasks affect the performance of the steps in the knowledge workers process?
<--- Score

101. Who gets your output?
<--- Score

102. What training and qualifications will you need?
<--- Score

103. How do you implement and manage your work processes to ensure that they meet design requirements?
<--- Score

104. What controls do you have in place to protect data?
<--- Score

105. How has the knowledge workers data been gathered?
<--- Score

106. How do mission and objectives affect the knowledge workers processes of your organization?
<--- Score

107. What is the Value Stream Mapping?
<--- Score

108. Who is involved with workflow mapping?
<--- Score

109. How do you ensure that the knowledge workers opportunity is realistic?
<--- Score

110. How will the change process be managed?
<--- Score

111. Which knowledge workers data should be retained?
<--- Score

112. What methods do you use to gather knowledge workers data?
<--- Score

113. Has data output been validated?
<--- Score

114. What quality tools were used to get through the analyze phase?
<--- Score

115. How will the knowledge workers data be captured?
<--- Score

116. What is the oversight process?
<--- Score

117. What tools were used to generate the list of possible causes?
<--- Score

118. What are the revised rough estimates of the financial savings/opportunity for knowledge workers improvements?
<--- Score

119. How can risk management be tied procedurally to process elements?
<--- Score

120. What qualifications are necessary?
<--- Score

121. What information qualified as important?
<--- Score

122. What knowledge workers data will be collected?
<--- Score

123. How do you define collaboration and team output?
<--- Score

124. How will the data be checked for quality?
<--- Score

125. Do several people in different organizational units assist with the knowledge workers process?
<--- Score

126. What knowledge workers data should be managed?
<--- Score

127. Can you add value to the current knowledge workers decision-making process (largely qualitative) by incorporating uncertainty modeling (more quantitative)?
<--- Score

128. Who owns what data?
<--- Score

129. How is data used for program management and improvement?
<--- Score

130. What, related to, knowledge workers processes does your organization outsource?
<--- Score

131. How much data can be collected in the given timeframe?
<--- Score

132. Is pre-qualification of suppliers carried out?
<--- Score

133. What conclusions were drawn from the team's data collection and analysis? How did the team reach these conclusions?
<--- Score

134. What technology breakthroughs will occur to empower knowledge workers and reduce operational data access requirements?
<--- Score

135. What process should you select for

improvement?

<--- Score

136. What types of data do your knowledge workers indicators require?

<--- Score

Add up total points for this section:

_ _ _ _ _ = Total points for this section

Divided by: _ _ _ _ _ _ (number of statements answered) = _ _ _ _ _ _ Average score for this section

Transfer your score to the knowledge workers Index at the beginning of the Self-Assessment.

CRITERION #5: IMPROVE:

INTENT: Develop a practical solution. Innovate, establish and test the solution and to measure the results.

In my belief, the answer to this question is clearly defined:

5 Strongly Agree

4 Agree

3 Neutral

2 Disagree

1 Strongly Disagree

1. What went well, what should change, what can improve?
<--- Score

2. What strategies for knowledge workers improvement are successful?
<--- Score

3. What is the magnitude of the improvements?

<--- Score

4. What are the expected knowledge workers results?
<--- Score

5. What tools were most useful during the improve phase?
<--- Score

6. Who will be responsible for making the decisions to include or exclude requested changes once knowledge workers is underway?
<--- Score

7. Who are the knowledge workers decision-makers?
<--- Score

8. Risk Identification: What are the possible risk events your organization faces in relation to knowledge workers?
<--- Score

9. How is continuous improvement applied to risk management?
<--- Score

10. Who manages knowledge workers risk?
<--- Score

11. What practices helps your organization to develop its capacity to recognize patterns?
<--- Score

12. Do you combine technical expertise with business knowledge and knowledge workers Key topics include lifecycles, development approaches,

requirements and how to make a business case?
<--- Score

13. Are the most efficient solutions problem-specific?
<--- Score

14. What is knowledge workers's impact on utilizing the best solution(s)?
<--- Score

15. What is knowledge workers risk?
<--- Score

16. Are the key business and technology risks being managed?
<--- Score

17. Who should make the knowledge workers decisions?
<--- Score

18. When you map the key players in your own work and the types/domains of relationships with them, which relationships do you find easy and which challenging, and why?
<--- Score

19. How do you deal with knowledge workers risk?
<--- Score

20. Who are the knowledge workers decision makers?
<--- Score

21. Where do the knowledge workers decisions reside?
<--- Score

22. For decision problems, how do you develop a decision statement?
<--- Score

23. Would you develop a knowledge workers Communication Strategy?
<--- Score

24. How can you better manage risk?
<--- Score

25. Have you identified breakpoints and/or risk tolerances that will trigger broad consideration of a potential need for intervention or modification of strategy?
<--- Score

26. How does the team improve its work?
<--- Score

27. How can the phases of knowledge workers development be identified?
<--- Score

28. Do you have the optimal project management team structure?
<--- Score

29. Is risk periodically assessed?
<--- Score

30. What lessons, if any, from a pilot were incorporated into the design of the full-scale solution?
<--- Score

31. How will you know that you have improved?
<--- Score

32. What alternative responses are available to manage risk?
<--- Score

33. How will you measure the results?
<--- Score

34. Where do you need knowledge workers improvement?
<--- Score

35. knowledge workers risk decisions: whose call Is It?
<--- Score

36. How risky is your organization?
<--- Score

37. Who controls the risk?
<--- Score

38. What improvements have been achieved?
<--- Score

39. What tools were used to evaluate the potential solutions?
<--- Score

40. In the past few months, what is the smallest change you have made that has had the biggest positive result? What was it about that small change that produced the large return?
<--- Score

41. Who do you report knowledge workers results to?
<--- Score

42. How do you measure risk?
<--- Score

43. How do you link measurement and risk?
<--- Score

44. Is any knowledge workers documentation required?
<--- Score

45. How are policy decisions made and where?
<--- Score

46. To what extent does management recognize knowledge workers as a tool to increase the results?
<--- Score

47. How can you improve performance?
<--- Score

48. How scalable is your knowledge workers solution?
<--- Score

49. If you could go back in time five years, what decision would you make differently? What is your best guess as to what decision you're making today you might regret five years from now?
<--- Score

50. What tools do you use once you have decided on a knowledge workers strategy and more importantly how do you choose?
<--- Score

51. What were the criteria for evaluating a knowledge workers pilot?
<--- Score

52. What are the concrete knowledge workers results?
<--- Score

53. Is the knowledge workers risk managed?
<--- Score

54. What needs improvement? Why?
<--- Score

55. What do you want to improve?
<--- Score

56. How do you go about comparing knowledge workers approaches/solutions?
<--- Score

57. Have you achieved knowledge workers improvements?
<--- Score

58. Do you need to do a usability evaluation?
<--- Score

59. Are the risks fully understood, reasonable and manageable?
<--- Score

60. Is knowledge workers documentation maintained?
<--- Score

61. How do you improve productivity?

<--- Score

62. Which of the recognised risks out of all risks can be most likely transferred?
<--- Score

63. What are the implications of the one critical knowledge workers decision 10 minutes, 10 months, and 10 years from now?
<--- Score

64. Explorations of the frontiers of knowledge workers will help you build influence, improve knowledge workers, optimize decision making, and sustain change, what is your approach?
<--- Score

65. Is there a high likelihood that any recommendations will achieve their intended results?
<--- Score

66. Is the knowledge workers documentation thorough?
<--- Score

67. What area needs the greatest improvement?
<--- Score

68. How do you manage and improve your knowledge workers work systems to deliver customer value and achieve organizational success and sustainability?
<--- Score

69. What were the underlying assumptions on the cost-benefit analysis?

<--- Score

70. What communications are necessary to support the implementation of the solution?
<--- Score

71. How do the knowledge workers results compare with the performance of your competitors and other organizations with similar offerings?
<--- Score

72. Is there any other knowledge workers solution?
<--- Score

73. For estimation problems, how do you develop an estimation statement?
<--- Score

74. How are knowledge workers risks managed?
<--- Score

75. What knowledge workers improvements can be made?
<--- Score

76. Do you cover the five essential competencies: Communication, Collaboration,Innovation, Adaptability, and Leadership that improve an organizations ability to leverage the new knowledge workers in a volatile global economy?
<--- Score

77. Will the controls trigger any other risks?
<--- Score

78. Is the measure of success for knowledge workers

understandable to a variety of people?
<--- Score

79. Are events managed to resolution?
<--- Score

80. Does the goal represent a desired result that can be measured?
<--- Score

81. What does the 'should be' process map/design look like?
<--- Score

82. How will you know that a change is an improvement?
<--- Score

83. How significant is the improvement in the eyes of the end user?
<--- Score

84. Do vendor agreements bring new compliance risk ?
<--- Score

85. What are your current levels and trends in key measures or indicators of workforce and leader development?
<--- Score

86. Are you assessing knowledge workers and risk?
<--- Score

87. Can you identify any significant risks or exposures to knowledge workers third- parties (vendors, service

providers, alliance partners etc) that concern you?
<--- Score

88. What attendant changes will need to be made to ensure that the solution is successful?
<--- Score

89. Was a knowledge workers charter developed?
<--- Score

90. Is supporting knowledge workers documentation required?
<--- Score

91. How do you define the solutions' scope?
<--- Score

92. How does your organization evaluate strategic knowledge workers success?
<--- Score

93. How will you recognize and celebrate results?
<--- Score

94. Are procedures documented for managing knowledge workers risks?
<--- Score

95. Why improve in the first place?
<--- Score

96. How do you improve your likelihood of success ?
<--- Score

97. Who makes the knowledge workers decisions in your organization?

<--- Score

98. Risk events: what are the things that could go wrong?
<--- Score

99. What is the risk?
<--- Score

100. What is the knowledge workers's sustainability risk?
<--- Score

101. What are the knowledge workers security risks?
<--- Score

102. What assumptions are made about the solution and approach?
<--- Score

103. What to do with the results or outcomes of measurements?
<--- Score

104. How do you decide how much to remunerate an employee?
<--- Score

105. Who are the key stakeholders for the knowledge workers evaluation?
<--- Score

106. Is the knowledge workers solution sustainable?
<--- Score

107. Who are the people involved in developing and

implementing knowledge workers?
<--- Score

108. Who will be responsible for documenting the knowledge workers requirements in detail?
<--- Score

109. Who manages supplier risk management in your organization?
<--- Score

110. What is the implementation plan?
<--- Score

111. How do you manage knowledge workers risk?
<--- Score

112. At what point will vulnerability assessments be performed once knowledge workers is put into production (e.g., ongoing Risk Management after implementation)?
<--- Score

113. Are risk management tasks balanced centrally and locally?
<--- Score

114. What can you do to improve?
<--- Score

115. What actually has to improve and by how much?
<--- Score

116. What error proofing will be done to address some of the discrepancies observed in the 'as is' process?
<--- Score

117. Which knowledge workers solution is appropriate?
<--- Score

118. What risks do you need to manage?
<--- Score

119. Do those selected for the knowledge workers team have a good general understanding of what knowledge workers is all about?
<--- Score

120. How can you improve knowledge workers?
<--- Score

121. Who will be using the results of the measurement activities?
<--- Score

122. What tools were used to tap into the creativity and encourage 'outside the box' thinking?
<--- Score

123. How do you measure progress and evaluate training effectiveness?
<--- Score

124. Can you integrate quality management and risk management?
<--- Score

125. What should a proof of concept or pilot accomplish?
<--- Score

126. What resources are required for the improvement efforts?
<--- Score

127. How is knowledge sharing about risk management improved?
<--- Score

128. What criteria will you use to assess your knowledge workers risks?
<--- Score

129. What is the team's contingency plan for potential problems occurring in implementation?
<--- Score

130. Is the solution technically practical?
<--- Score

131. Is the scope clearly documented?
<--- Score

132. Does a good decision guarantee a good outcome?
<--- Score

133. How do you improve knowledge workers service perception, and satisfaction?
<--- Score

134. Are risk triggers captured?
<--- Score

135. How will you know when its improved?
<--- Score

Add up total points for this section:
_____ = Total points for this section

Divided by: _____ (number of
statements answered) = _____
Average score for this section

Transfer your score to the knowledge
workers Index at the beginning of the
Self-Assessment.

CRITERION #6: CONTROL:

INTENT: Implement the practical solution. Maintain the performance and correct possible complications.

In my belief, the answer to this question is clearly defined:

5 Strongly Agree

4 Agree

3 Neutral

2 Disagree

1 Strongly Disagree

1. Is there a knowledge workers Communication plan covering who needs to get what information when?
<--- Score

2. Are suggested corrective/restorative actions indicated on the response plan for known causes to problems that might surface?
<--- Score

3. In the case of a knowledge workers project, the criteria for the audit derive from implementation objectives, an audit of a knowledge workers project involves assessing whether the recommendations outlined for implementation have been met, can you track that any knowledge workers project is implemented as planned, and is it working?
<--- Score

4. What should the next improvement project be that is related to knowledge workers?
<--- Score

5. How likely is the current knowledge workers plan to come in on schedule or on budget?
<--- Score

6. Is there an action plan in case of emergencies?
<--- Score

7. What knowledge workers standards are applicable?
<--- Score

8. Who controls critical resources?
<--- Score

9. What is the best design framework for knowledge workers organization now that, in a post industrial-age if the top-down, command and control model is no longer relevant?
<--- Score

10. What is your plan to assess your security risks?
<--- Score

11. Are you measuring, monitoring and predicting

knowledge workers activities to optimize operations and profitability, and enhancing outcomes?
<--- Score

12. Have new or revised work instructions resulted?
<--- Score

13. What are your results for key measures or indicators of the accomplishment of your knowledge workers strategy and action plans, including building and strengthening core competencies?
<--- Score

14. What are the critical parameters to watch?
<--- Score

15. Does the knowledge workers performance meet the customer's requirements?
<--- Score

16. Are the planned controls working?
<--- Score

17. Who is going to spread your message?
<--- Score

18. What do you measure to verify effectiveness gains?
<--- Score

19. What should you measure to verify efficiency gains?
<--- Score

20. Do you monitor the effectiveness of your knowledge workers activities?

<--- Score

21. What is your theory of human motivation, and how does your compensation plan fit with that view?
<--- Score

22. Is there a standardized process?
<--- Score

23. Who will be in control?
<--- Score

24. Does knowledge workers appropriately measure and monitor risk?
<--- Score

25. What do your reports reflect?
<--- Score

26. Does a troubleshooting guide exist or is it needed?
<--- Score

27. Has the improved process and its steps been standardized?
<--- Score

28. Is a response plan in place for when the input, process, or output measures indicate an 'out-of-control' condition?
<--- Score

29. Are there documented procedures?
<--- Score

30. How do your controls stack up?
<--- Score

31. How will you measure your QA plan's effectiveness?
<--- Score

32. How will the process owner verify improvement in present and future sigma levels, process capabilities?
<--- Score

33. How might the group capture best practices and lessons learned so as to leverage improvements?
<--- Score

34. Is a response plan established and deployed?
<--- Score

35. How do you monitor usage and cost?
<--- Score

36. How can you best use all of your knowledge repositories to enhance learning and sharing?
<--- Score

37. How widespread is its use?
<--- Score

38. What are you attempting to measure/monitor?
<--- Score

39. Does job training on the documented procedures need to be part of the process team's education and training?
<--- Score

40. What is the recommended frequency of auditing?
<--- Score

41. Is there a documented and implemented monitoring plan?
<--- Score

42. Will existing staff require re-training, for example, to learn new business processes?
<--- Score

43. Are pertinent alerts monitored, analyzed and distributed to appropriate personnel?
<--- Score

44. Are new process steps, standards, and documentation ingrained into normal operations?
<--- Score

45. What are the known security controls?
<--- Score

46. What adjustments to the strategies are needed?
<--- Score

47. Do the viable solutions scale to future needs?
<--- Score

48. Does the response plan contain a definite closed loop continual improvement scheme (e.g., plan-do-check-act)?
<--- Score

49. How do controls support value?
<--- Score

50. Who has control over resources?
<--- Score

51. What are the key elements of your knowledge workers performance improvement system, including your evaluation, organizational learning, and innovation processes?
<--- Score

52. What quality tools were useful in the control phase?
<--- Score

53. Are the knowledge workers standards challenging?
<--- Score

54. What key inputs and outputs are being measured on an ongoing basis?
<--- Score

55. Do the knowledge workers decisions you make today help people and the planet tomorrow?
<--- Score

56. Are documented procedures clear and easy to follow for the operators?
<--- Score

57. What is the standard for acceptable knowledge workers performance?
<--- Score

58. What are customers monitoring?
<--- Score

59. Is reporting being used or needed?
<--- Score

60. Is there documentation that will support the successful operation of the improvement?
<--- Score

61. What other systems, operations, processes, and infrastructures (hiring practices, staffing, training, incentives/rewards, metrics/dashboards/scorecards, etc.) need updates, additions, changes, or deletions in order to facilitate knowledge transfer and improvements?
<--- Score

62. Act/Adjust: What Do you Need to Do Differently?
<--- Score

63. Is knowledge gained on process shared and institutionalized?
<--- Score

64. Is new knowledge gained imbedded in the response plan?
<--- Score

65. Where do ideas that reach policy makers and planners as proposals for knowledge workers strengthening and reform actually originate?
<--- Score

66. Against what alternative is success being measured?
<--- Score

67. Implementation Planning: is a pilot needed to test the changes before a full roll out occurs?
<--- Score

68. What is the control/monitoring plan?
<--- Score

69. Has the knowledge workers value of standards been quantified?
<--- Score

70. How will knowledge workers decisions be made and monitored?
<--- Score

71. How do you plan for the cost of succession?
<--- Score

72. Will any special training be provided for results interpretation?
<--- Score

73. Will your goals reflect your program budget?
<--- Score

74. How will input, process, and output variables be checked to detect for sub-optimal conditions?
<--- Score

75. How is knowledge workers project cost planned, managed, monitored?
<--- Score

76. How will the day-to-day responsibilities for monitoring and continual improvement be transferred from the improvement team to the process owner?
<--- Score

77. What can you control?
<--- Score

78. How will the process owner and team be able to hold the gains?
<--- Score

79. Are operating procedures consistent?
<--- Score

80. Is there a recommended audit plan for routine surveillance inspections of knowledge workers's gains?
<--- Score

81. Is there a control plan in place for sustaining improvements (short and long-term)?
<--- Score

82. How do senior leaders actions reflect a commitment to the organizations knowledge workers values?
<--- Score

83. Who is the knowledge workers process owner?
<--- Score

84. Is the knowledge workers test/monitoring cost justified?
<--- Score

85. Can you adapt and adjust to changing knowledge workers situations?
<--- Score

86. Is there a transfer of ownership and knowledge

to process owner and process team tasked with the responsibilities.
<--- Score

87. Are the planned controls in place?
<--- Score

88. What are the performance and scale of the knowledge workers tools?
<--- Score

89. Are controls in place and consistently applied?
<--- Score

90. How do you spread information?
<--- Score

91. How do you encourage people to take control and responsibility?
<--- Score

92. How will report readings be checked to effectively monitor performance?
<--- Score

93. What other areas of the group might benefit from the knowledge workers team's improvements, knowledge, and learning?
<--- Score

94. How will new or emerging customer needs/ requirements be checked/communicated to orient the process toward meeting the new specifications and continually reducing variation?
<--- Score

95. Do you monitor the knowledge workers decisions made and fine tune them as they evolve?
<--- Score

96. Can support from partners be adjusted?
<--- Score

97. How do you select, collect, align, and integrate knowledge workers data and information for tracking daily operations and overall organizational performance, including progress relative to strategic objectives and action plans?
<--- Score

Add up total points for this section:
_ _ _ _ _ = Total points for this section

Divided by: _ _ _ _ _ _ (number of statements answered) = _ _ _ _ _ _
Average score for this section

Transfer your score to the knowledge workers Index at the beginning of the Self-Assessment.

CRITERION #7: SUSTAIN:

INTENT: Retain the benefits.

In my belief, the answer to this question is clearly defined:

5 Strongly Agree

4 Agree

3 Neutral

2 Disagree

1 Strongly Disagree

1. How do you accomplish your long range knowledge workers goals?
<--- Score

2. Can the schedule be done in the given time?
<--- Score

3. Can you maintain your growth without detracting from the factors that have contributed to your success?
<--- Score

4. Why not do knowledge workers?
<--- Score

5. Ask yourself: how would you do this work if you only had one staff member to do it?
<--- Score

6. How do you transition from the baseline to the target?
<--- Score

7. Whom among your colleagues do you trust, and for what?
<--- Score

8. How do you set knowledge workers stretch targets and how do you get people to not only participate in setting these stretch targets but also that they strive to achieve these?
<--- Score

9. Where can you break convention?
<--- Score

10. Do you think you know, or do you know you know ?
<--- Score

11. What trouble can you get into?
<--- Score

12. Knowledge workers are now untethered, able to perform tasks anywhere at any time. What do the best of them want from your organization?
<--- Score

13. Is there any existing knowledge workers governance structure?
<--- Score

14. Is knowledge workers dependent on the successful delivery of a current project?
<--- Score

15. What is a feasible sequencing of reform initiatives over time?
<--- Score

16. If your company went out of business tomorrow, would anyone who doesn't get a paycheck here care?
<--- Score

17. How do you keep the momentum going?
<--- Score

18. Who do we want your customers to become?
<--- Score

19. What are the business goals knowledge workers is aiming to achieve?
<--- Score

20. How do you maintain knowledge workers's Integrity?
<--- Score

21. How do senior leaders deploy your organizations vision and values through your leadership system, to the workforce, to key suppliers and partners, and to customers and other stakeholders, as appropriate?
<--- Score

22. How will you insure seamless interoperability of knowledge workers moving forward?
<--- Score

23. What are internal and external knowledge workers relations?
<--- Score

24. Whose voice (department, ethnic group, women, older workers, etc) might you have missed hearing from in your company, and how might you amplify this voice to create positive momentum for your business?
<--- Score

25. What are specific knowledge workers rules to follow?
<--- Score

26. Which individuals, teams or departments will be involved in knowledge workers?
<--- Score

27. What are the rules and assumptions your industry operates under? What if the opposite were true?
<--- Score

28. What is the kind of project structure that would be appropriate for your knowledge workers project, should it be formal and complex, or can it be less formal and relatively simple?
<--- Score

29. What information is critical to your organization that your executives are ignoring?

<--- Score

30. What trophy do you want on your mantle?
<--- Score

31. Why is it important to have senior management support for a knowledge workers project?
<--- Score

32. If you weren't already in this business, would you enter it today? And if not, what are you going to do about it?
<--- Score

33. What do you believe holds back knowledge workers in your organization?
<--- Score

34. What potential megatrends could make your business model obsolete?
<--- Score

35. What was the last experiment you ran?
<--- Score

36. How can you become the company that would put you out of business?
<--- Score

37. Will there be any necessary staff changes (redundancies or new hires)?
<--- Score

38. What knowledge, skills and characteristics mark a good knowledge workers project manager?
<--- Score

39. What are you challenging?
<--- Score

40. What knowledge workers skills are most important?
<--- Score

41. How do you deal with knowledge workers changes?
<--- Score

42. What will be the consequences to the stakeholder (financial, reputation etc) if knowledge workers does not go ahead or fails to deliver the objectives?
<--- Score

43. What are the success criteria that will indicate that knowledge workers objectives have been met and the benefits delivered?
<--- Score

44. What is your BATNA (best alternative to a negotiated agreement)?
<--- Score

45. What are the long-term knowledge workers goals?
<--- Score

46. How will you know that the knowledge workers project has been successful?
<--- Score

47. Is a knowledge workers team work effort in place?
<--- Score

48. Who uses your product in ways you never expected?
<--- Score

49. What are the key enablers to make this knowledge workers move?
<--- Score

50. Why do and why don't your customers like your organization?
<--- Score

51. What are the challenges?
<--- Score

52. Do you say no to customers for no reason?
<--- Score

53. How will you motivate the stakeholders with the least vested interest?
<--- Score

54. How are you doing compared to your industry?
<--- Score

55. How do you stay inspired?
<--- Score

56. How important is knowledge workers to the user organizations mission?
<--- Score

57. How do you make it meaningful in connecting knowledge workers with what users do day-to-day?
<--- Score

58. What is an unauthorized commitment?
<--- Score

59. What are your most important goals for the strategic knowledge workers objectives?
<--- Score

60. What have been your experiences in defining long range knowledge workers goals?
<--- Score

61. How do you proactively clarify deliverables and knowledge workers quality expectations?
<--- Score

62. What have you done to protect your business from competitive encroachment?
<--- Score

63. How do you track customer value, profitability or financial return, organizational success, and sustainability?
<--- Score

64. Did your employees make progress today?
<--- Score

65. Are you maintaining a past–present–future perspective throughout the knowledge workers discussion?
<--- Score

66. What are the potential basics of knowledge workers fraud?
<--- Score

67. To whom do you add value?
<--- Score

68. Are assumptions made in knowledge workers stated explicitly?
<--- Score

69. How much contingency will be available in the budget?
<--- Score

70. Is the knowledge workers organization completing tasks effectively and efficiently?
<--- Score

71. What is something you believe that nearly no one agrees with you on?
<--- Score

72. Who have you, as a company, historically been when you've been at your best?
<--- Score

73. Who are the key stakeholders?
<--- Score

74. What business benefits will knowledge workers goals deliver if achieved?
<--- Score

75. If you got fired and a new hire took your place, what would she do different?
<--- Score

76. Does that mean that knowledge workers are located everywhere?

<--- Score

77. How can you become more high-tech but still be high touch?
<--- Score

78. What does your signature ensure?
<--- Score

79. What are strategies for increasing support and reducing opposition?
<--- Score

80. Do you have highly paid knowledge workers dedicated to time-consuming administrative tasks?
<--- Score

81. Is your basic point _____ or _____?
<--- Score

82. What counts that you are not counting?
<--- Score

83. Who is on the team?
<--- Score

84. What is the source of the strategies for knowledge workers strengthening and reform?
<--- Score

85. If no one would ever find out about your accomplishments, how would you lead differently?
<--- Score

86. Marketing budgets are tighter, consumers are

more skeptical, and social media has changed forever the way we talk about knowledge workers, how do you gain traction?
<--- Score

87. What would have to be true for the option on the table to be the best possible choice?
<--- Score

88. Political -is anyone trying to undermine this project?
<--- Score

89. What knowledge workers modifications can you make work for you?
<--- Score

90. Will it be accepted by users?
<--- Score

91. If your customer were your grandmother, would you tell her to buy what you're selling?
<--- Score

92. How do you foster the skills, knowledge, talents, attributes, and characteristics you want to have?
<--- Score

93. Can you do all this work?
<--- Score

94. Who will determine interim and final deadlines?
<--- Score

95. Do you have enough freaky customers in your portfolio pushing you to the limit day in and day out?

<--- Score

96. What are your personal philosophies regarding knowledge workers and how do they influence your work?
<--- Score

97. How do you create buy-in?
<--- Score

98. How do you govern and fulfill your societal responsibilities?
<--- Score

99. Do you feel that more should be done in the knowledge workers area?
<--- Score

100. What may be the consequences for the performance of an organization if all stakeholders are not consulted regarding knowledge workers?
<--- Score

101. What are the essentials of internal knowledge workers management?
<--- Score

102. What one word do you want to own in the minds of your customers, employees, and partners?
<--- Score

103. What is the overall business strategy?
<--- Score

104. Is your strategy driving your strategy? Or is the way in which you allocate resources driving your

strategy?

<--- Score

105. What is effective knowledge workers?

<--- Score

106. Is there a work around that you can use?

<--- Score

107. Which functions and people interact with the supplier and or customer?

<--- Score

108. What happens if you do not have enough funding?

<--- Score

109. Is knowledge workers realistic, or are you setting yourself up for failure?

<--- Score

110. If there were zero limitations, what would you do differently?

<--- Score

111. Is there a shortage of knowledge workers?

<--- Score

112. How is implementation research currently incorporated into each of your goals?

<--- Score

113. Who do you want your customers to become?

<--- Score

114. Why is knowledge workers important for you

now?
<--- Score

115. Who is responsible for knowledge workers?
<--- Score

116. Which models, tools and techniques are necessary?
<--- Score

117. How likely is it that a customer would recommend your company to a friend or colleague?
<--- Score

118. How can you incorporate support to ensure safe and effective use of knowledge workers into the services that you provide?
<--- Score

119. Do you see more potential in people than they do in themselves?
<--- Score

120. What are the short and long-term knowledge workers goals?
<--- Score

121. What is in IT for knowledge workers?
<--- Score

122. If you had to leave your organization for a year and the only communication you could have with employees/colleagues was a single paragraph, what would you write?
<--- Score

123. Who else should you help?
<--- Score

124. What are the barriers to increased knowledge workers production?
<--- Score

125. What is the overall talent health of your organization as a whole at senior levels, and for each organization reporting to a member of the Senior Leadership Team?
<--- Score

126. What stupid rule would you most like to kill?
<--- Score

127. Do you have the right people on the bus?
<--- Score

128. Who is the main stakeholder, with ultimate responsibility for driving knowledge workers forward?
<--- Score

129. What is it like to work for you?
<--- Score

130. What are you trying to prove to yourself, and how might it be hijacking your life and business success?
<--- Score

131. What is the range of capabilities?
<--- Score

132. Who do you think the world wants your organization to be?
<--- Score

133. How do customers see your organization?
<--- Score

134. Which knowledge workers goals are the most important?
<--- Score

135. Who are four people whose careers you have enhanced?
<--- Score

136. What is your competitive advantage?
<--- Score

137. How can you negotiate knowledge workers successfully with a stubborn boss, an irate client, or a deceitful coworker?
<--- Score

138. How do you go about securing knowledge workers?
<--- Score

139. What happens when a new employee joins the organization?
<--- Score

140. What could happen if you do not do it?
<--- Score

141. How do you engage the workforce, in addition to satisfying them?
<--- Score

142. How do you ensure that implementations of

knowledge workers products are done in a way that ensures safety?
<--- Score

143. In the past year, what have you done (or could you have done) to increase the accurate perception of your company/brand as ethical and honest?
<--- Score

144. In a project to restructure knowledge workers outcomes, which stakeholders would you involve?
<--- Score

145. Are you making progress, and are you making progress as knowledge workers leaders?
<--- Score

146. What happens at your organization when people fail?
<--- Score

147. Who are your customers?
<--- Score

148. How will you ensure you get what you expected?
<--- Score

149. Who is responsible for errors?
<--- Score

150. Who will provide the final approval of knowledge workers deliverables?
<--- Score

151. What is the recommended frequency of auditing?
<--- Score

152. What would you recommend your friend do if he/ she were facing this dilemma?
<--- Score

153. Are you using a design thinking approach and integrating Innovation, knowledge workers Experience, and Brand Value?
<--- Score

154. If you were responsible for initiating and implementing major changes in your organization, what steps might you take to ensure acceptance of those changes?
<--- Score

155. Who, on the executive team or the board, has spoken to a customer recently?
<--- Score

156. What unique value proposition (UVP) do you offer?
<--- Score

157. What is the estimated value of the project?
<--- Score

158. Operational - will it work?
<--- Score

159. What are current knowledge workers paradigms?
<--- Score

160. How long will it take to change?
<--- Score

161. Think of your knowledge workers project, what are the main functions?
<--- Score

162. What did you miss in the interview for the worst hire you ever made?
<--- Score

163. Do you know what you are doing? And who do you call if you don't?
<--- Score

164. Would you rather sell to knowledgeable and informed customers or to uninformed customers?
<--- Score

165. If you do not follow, then how to lead?
<--- Score

166. What is your question? Why?
<--- Score

167. Are the assumptions believable and achievable?
<--- Score

168. How do you determine the key elements that affect knowledge workers workforce satisfaction, how are these elements determined for different workforce groups and segments?
<--- Score

169. What is the purpose of knowledge workers in relation to the mission?
<--- Score

170. What are the top 3 things at the forefront of your

knowledge workers agendas for the next 3 years?
<--- Score

171. Are you / should you be revolutionary or evolutionary?
<--- Score

172. What relationships among knowledge workers trends do you perceive?
<--- Score

173. Do you have past knowledge workers successes?
<--- Score

174. What projects are going on in the organization today, and what resources are those projects using from the resource pools?
<--- Score

175. What management system can you use to leverage the knowledge workers experience, ideas, and concerns of the people closest to the work to be done?
<--- Score

176. Is it economical; do you have the time and money?
<--- Score

177. Do you think knowledge workers accomplishes the goals you expect it to accomplish?
<--- Score

178. Who is responsible for ensuring appropriate resources (time, people and money) are allocated to knowledge workers?

<--- Score

179. What role does communication play in the success or failure of a knowledge workers project?
<--- Score

180. How do you keep records, of what?
<--- Score

181. If you had to rebuild your organization without any traditional competitive advantages (i.e., no killer technology, promising research, innovative product/ service delivery model, etcetera), how would your people have to approach their work and collaborate together in order to create the necessary conditions for success?
<--- Score

182. How do you provide a safe environment -physically and emotionally?
<--- Score

183. Is maximizing knowledge workers protection the same as minimizing knowledge workers loss?
<--- Score

184. How do you manage knowledge workers Knowledge Management (KM)?
<--- Score

185. What you are going to do to affect the numbers?
<--- Score

186. How do you lead with knowledge workers in mind?
<--- Score

Add up total points for this section:

_____ = Total points for this section

Divided by: _____ (number of
statements answered) = _____
Average score for this section

Transfer your score to the knowledge
workers Index at the beginning of the
Self-Assessment.

Knowledge Workers and Managing Projects, Criteria for Project Managers:

1.0 Initiating Process Group: Knowledge Workers

1. At which stage, in a typical Knowledge Workers project do stake holders have maximum influence?

2. How well did you do?

3. What areas does the group agree are the biggest success on the Knowledge Workers project?

4. Do you know all the stakeholders impacted by the Knowledge Workers project and what needs are?

5. Who is behind the Knowledge Workers project?

6. How to control and approve each phase?

7. What are the inputs required to produce the deliverables?

8. Do you know the Knowledge Workers projects goal, purpose and objectives?

9. In which Knowledge Workers project management process group is the detailed Knowledge Workers project budget created?

10. Who is involved in each phase?

11. Have requirements been tested, approved, and fulfill the Knowledge Workers project scope?

12. What are the tools and techniques to be used in each phase?

13. During which stage of Risk planning are risks prioritized based on probability and impact?

14. Did the Knowledge Workers project team have the right skills?

15. The Knowledge Workers project you are managing has nine stakeholders. How many channel of communications are there between corresponding stakeholders?

16. Measurable - are the targets measurable?

17. What are the constraints?

18. If the risk event occurs, what will you do?

19. Do you understand the communication expectations for this Knowledge Workers project?

20. What will you do?

1.1 Project Charter: Knowledge Workers

21. Market – identify products market, including whether it is outside of the objective: what is the purpose of the program or Knowledge Workers project?

22. Fit with other Products Compliments – Cannibalizes?

23. What ideas do you have for initial tests of change (PDSA cycles)?

24. Why have you chosen the aim you have set forth?

25. Are there special technology requirements?

26. Why the improvements?

27. Where and how does the team fit within your organization structure?

28. Success determination factors: how will the success of the Knowledge Workers project be determined from the customers perspective?

29. If finished, on what date did it finish?

30. What are some examples of a business case?

31. What metrics could you look at?

32. What are the assumptions?

33. Run it as as a startup?

34. What are you trying to accomplish?

35. How much?

36. How high should you set your goals?

37. What are you striving to accomplish (measurable goal(s))?

38. What are the known stakeholder requirements?

39. How will you know a change is an improvement?

1.2 Stakeholder Register: Knowledge Workers

40. What opportunities exist to provide communications?

41. Is your organization ready for change?

42. How should employers make voices heard?

43. How much influence do they have on the Knowledge Workers project?

44. How big is the gap?

45. What is the power of the stakeholder?

46. Who is managing stakeholder engagement?

47. What & Why?

48. Who wants to talk about Security?

49. Who are the stakeholders?

50. How will reports be created?

51. What are the major Knowledge Workers project milestones requiring communications or providing communications opportunities?

1.3 Stakeholder Analysis Matrix: Knowledge Workers

52. What is relationship with the Knowledge Workers project?

53. Which conditions out of the control of the management are crucial for the sustainability of its effects?

54. Vulnerable groups; who are the vulnerable groups that might be affected by the Knowledge Workers project?

55. Alliances: with which other actors is the actor allied, how are they interconnected?

56. Competitor intentions - various?

57. Does the stakeholder want to be involved or merely need to be informed about the Knowledge Workers project and its process?

58. What can the stakeholder prevent from happening?

59. How are the threatened Knowledge Workers project targets being used?

60. Resources, assets, people?

61. What could your organization improve?

62. Who is directly responsible for decisions on issues important to the Knowledge Workers project?

63. Who influences whom?

64. How can you fill the need to show progress?

65. Industry or lifestyle trends?

66. What mechanisms are proposed to monitor and measure Knowledge Workers project performance in terms of social development outcomes?

67. How can you counter negative efforts?

68. Competitors vulnerabilities?

69. Are you going to weigh the stakeholders?

70. What is the stakeholders mandate, what is mission?

71. If you can not fix it, how do you do it differently?

2.0 Planning Process Group: Knowledge Workers

72. If a risk event occurs, what will you do?

73. Is the Knowledge Workers project making progress in helping to achieve the set results?

74. When developing the estimates for Knowledge Workers project phases, you choose to add the individual estimates for the activities that comprise each phase. What type of estimation method are you using?

75. Is the Knowledge Workers project supported by national and/or local organizations?

76. What types of differentiated effects are resulting from the Knowledge Workers project and to what extent?

77. What business situation is being addressed?

78. In which Knowledge Workers project management process group is the detailed Knowledge Workers project budget created?

79. What good practices or successful experiences or transferable examples have been identified?

80. How should needs be met?

81. To what extent has a PMO contributed to raising

the quality of the design of the Knowledge Workers project?

82. First of all, should any action be taken?

83. If a task is partitionable, is this a sufficient condition to reduce the Knowledge Workers project duration?

84. How does activity resource estimation affect activity duration estimation?

85. Have operating capacities been created and/or reinforced in partners?

86. What makes your Knowledge Workers project successful?

87. To what extent are the visions and actions of the partners consistent or divergent with regard to the program?

88. How well will the chosen processes produce the expected results?

89. Mitigate. what will you do to minimize the impact should a risk event occur?

90. Is your organization showing technical capacity and leadership commitment to keep working with the Knowledge Workers project and to repeat it?

91. Product breakdown structure (pbs): what is the Knowledge Workers project result or product, and how should it look like, what are its parts?

2.1 Project Management Plan: Knowledge Workers

92. What worked well?

93. Is mitigation authorized or recommended?

94. If the Knowledge Workers project is complex or scope is specialized, do you have appropriate and/or qualified staff available to perform the tasks?

95. Was the peer (technical) review of the cost estimates duly coordinated with the cost estimate center of expertise and addressed in the review documentation and certification?

96. Does the implementation plan have an appropriate division of responsibilities?

97. Do there need to be organizational changes?

98. If the Knowledge Workers project management plan is a comprehensive document that guides you in Knowledge Workers project execution and control, then what should it NOT contain?

99. Development trends and opportunities. What if the positive direction and vision of your organization causes expected trends to change?

100. What is the justification?

101. When is a Knowledge Workers project

management plan created?

102. What did not work so well?

103. Why do you manage integration?

104. Are the proposed Knowledge Workers project purposes different than a previously authorized Knowledge Workers project?

105. Are there any windfall benefits that would accrue to the Knowledge Workers project sponsor or other parties?

106. How do you manage time?

107. What is the business need?

108. Did the planning effort collaborate to develop solutions that integrate expertise, policies, programs, and Knowledge Workers projects across entities?

109. Are there any Client staffing expectations?

110. Is there anything you would now do differently on your Knowledge Workers project based on past experience?

111. What is risk management?

2.2 Scope Management Plan: Knowledge Workers

112. Organizational policies that might affect the availability of resources?

113. Have the scope, objectives, costs, benefits and impacts been communicated to all involved and/or impacted stakeholders and work groups?

114. Is there an on-going process in place to monitor Knowledge Workers project risks?

115. Are the existing and future without-plan conditions reasonable and appropriate?

116. What are the risks that could significantly affect the scope of the Knowledge Workers project?

117. Is there a requirements change management processes in place?

118. Does the business case include how the Knowledge Workers project aligns with your organizations strategic goals & objectives?

119. Does the resource management plan include a personnel development plan?

120. Do you document disagreements and work towards resolutions?

121. Has allowance been made for vacations, holidays,

training (learning time for each team member), staff promotions & staff turnovers?

122. Timeline and milestones?

123. Describe the process for rejecting the Knowledge Workers project deliverables. What happens to rejected deliverables?

124. Has appropriate allowance been made for the effect of the learning curve on all personnel joining the Knowledge Workers project who do not have the required prior industry, functional & technical expertise?

125. What if you do not have more detailed information on the report?

126. Are actuals compared against estimates to analyze and correct variances?

127. Are alternatives safe, functional, constructible, economical, reasonable and sustainable?

128. Has adequate time for orientation & training of Knowledge Workers project staff been provided for in relation to technical nature of the application and the experience levels of Knowledge Workers project personnel?

129. Is there a formal set of procedures supporting Stakeholder Management?

130. Are meeting minutes captured and sent out after the meeting?

2.3 Requirements Management Plan: Knowledge Workers

131. When and how will a requirements baseline be established in this Knowledge Workers project?

132. How will the information be distributed?

133. Will you have access to stakeholders when you need them?

134. Who will approve the requirements (and if multiple approvers, in what order)?

135. Do you have an appropriate arrangement for meetings?

136. Who has the authority to reject Knowledge Workers project requirements?

137. Will the contractors involved take full responsibility?

138. Could inaccurate or incomplete requirements in this Knowledge Workers project create a serious risk for the business?

139. How will you develop the schedule of requirements activities?

140. Did you get proper approvals?

141. Subject to change control?

142. Is the user satisfied?

143. What is a problem?

144. Describe the process for rejecting the Knowledge Workers project requirements. Who has the authority to reject Knowledge Workers project requirements?

145. Who is responsible for monitoring and tracking the Knowledge Workers project requirements?

146. Do you know which stakeholders will participate in the requirements effort?

147. What are you counting on?

148. How will bidders price evaluations be done, by deliverables, phases, or in a big bang?

149. Do you expect stakeholders to be cooperative?

150. Who is responsible for quantifying the Knowledge Workers project requirements?

2.4 Requirements Documentation: Knowledge Workers

151. Can you check system requirements?

152. Are there any requirements conflicts?

153. Do your constraints stand?

154. How much testing do you need to do to prove that your system is safe?

155. What is a show stopper in the requirements?

156. How does what is being described meet the business need?

157. What facilities must be supported by the system?

158. Can the requirement be changed without a large impact on other requirements?

159. How do you know when a Requirement is accurate enough?

160. How will requirements be documented and who signs off on them?

161. What are the attributes of a customer?

162. Consistency. are there any requirements conflicts?

163. Is your business case still valid?

164. Are there legal issues?

165. Does your organization restrict technical alternatives?

166. What are the potential disadvantages/ advantages?

167. What will be the integration problems?

168. What is effective documentation?

169. Is the requirement realistically testable?

170. What kind of entity is a problem ?

2.5 Requirements Traceability Matrix: Knowledge Workers

171. Do you have a clear understanding of all subcontracts in place?

172. How do you manage scope?

173. What percentage of Knowledge Workers projects are producing traceability matrices between requirements and other work products?

174. Why do you manage scope?

175. How small is small enough?

176. Will you use a Requirements Traceability Matrix?

177. How will it affect the stakeholders personally in career?

178. Is there a requirements traceability process in place?

179. Describe the process for approving requirements so they can be added to the traceability matrix and Knowledge Workers project work can be performed. Will the Knowledge Workers project requirements become approved in writing?

180. What is the WBS?

181. Why use a WBS?

182. What are the chronologies, contingencies, consequences, criteria?

2.6 Project Scope Statement: Knowledge Workers

183. Will an issue form be in use?

184. Relevant - ask yourself can you get there; why are you doing this Knowledge Workers project?

185. Have you been able to easily identify success criteria and create objective measurements for each of the Knowledge Workers project scopes goal statements?

186. Will the risk plan be updated on a regular and frequent basis?

187. Write a brief purpose statement for this Knowledge Workers project. Include a business justification statement. What is the product of this Knowledge Workers project?

188. What is change?

189. Identify how your team and you will create the Knowledge Workers project scope statement and the work breakdown structure (WBS). Document how you will create the Knowledge Workers project scope statement and WBS, and make sure you answer the following questions: In defining Knowledge Workers project scope and the WBS, will you and your Knowledge Workers project team be using methods defined by your organization, methods defined by the Knowledge Workers project management office

(PMO), or other methods?

190. Did your Knowledge Workers project ask for this?

191. Change management vs. change leadership - what is the difference?

192. Have the reports to be produced, distributed, and filed been defined?

193. Are there adequate Knowledge Workers project control systems?

194. Who will you recommend approve the change, and when do you recommend the change reviews occur?

195. Any new risks introduced or old risks impacted. Are there issues that could affect the existing requirements for the result, service, or product if the scope changes?

196. What is a process you might recommend to verify the accuracy of the research deliverable?

197. Has a method and process for requirement tracking been developed?

198. Will statistics related to QA be collected, trends analyzed, and problems raised as issues?

199. Will tasks be marked complete only after QA has been successfully completed?

200. Will all Knowledge Workers project issues be unconditionally tracked through the issue resolution

process?

201. What are the defined meeting materials?

2.7 Assumption and Constraint Log: Knowledge Workers

202. Is the current scope of the Knowledge Workers project substantially different than that originally defined in the approved Knowledge Workers project plan?

203. Is this model reasonable?

204. How are new requirements or changes to requirements identified?

205. Model-building: what data-analytic strategies are useful when building proportional-hazards models?

206. How many Knowledge Workers project staff does this specific process affect?

207. When can log be discarded?

208. Have you eliminated all duplicative tasks or manual efforts, where appropriate?

209. Have adequate resources been provided by management to ensure Knowledge Workers project success?

210. How can you prevent/fix violations?

211. Have all necessary approvals been obtained?

212. Is staff trained on the software technologies that

are being used on the Knowledge Workers project?

213. Does the plan conform to standards?

214. Can you perform this task or activity in a more effective manner?

215. Does the traceability documentation describe the tool and/or mechanism to be used to capture traceability throughout the life cycle?

216. Are requirements management tracking tools and procedures in place?

217. Is the definition of the Knowledge Workers project scope clear; what needs to be accomplished?

218. Do the requirements meet the standards of correctness, completeness, consistency, accuracy, and readability?

219. Are there processes defining how software will be developed including development methods, overall timeline for development, software product standards, and traceability?

220. Are there processes in place to ensure internal consistency between the source code components?

2.8 Work Breakdown Structure: Knowledge Workers

221. When does it have to be done?

222. How will you and your Knowledge Workers project team define the Knowledge Workers projects scope and work breakdown structure?

223. Why would you develop a Work Breakdown Structure?

224. Do you need another level?

225. How far down?

226. How big is a work-package?

227. Is it still viable?

228. Who has to do it?

229. How much detail?

230. Where does it take place?

231. Is the work breakdown structure (wbs) defined and is the scope of the Knowledge Workers project clear with assigned deliverable owners?

232. Why is it useful?

233. When do you stop?

234. What has to be done?

235. When would you develop a Work Breakdown Structure?

236. How many levels?

237. Is it a change in scope?

2.9 WBS Dictionary: Knowledge Workers

238. Does the contractors system include procedures for measuring the performance of critical subcontractors?

239. Performance to date and material commitment?

240. Budgets assigned to control accounts?

241. Are overhead cost budgets established for each organization which has authority to incur overhead costs?

242. Are overhead budgets and costs being handled according to the disclosure statement when applicable, or otherwise properly classified (for example, engineering overhead, IR&D)?

243. Are all elements of indirect expense identified to overhead cost budgets of Knowledge Workers projections?

244. Are there procedures for monitoring action items and corrective actions to the point of resolution and are corresponding procedures being followed?

245. Are the bases and rates for allocating costs from each indirect pool to commercial work consistent with the already stated used to allocate corresponding costs to Government contracts?

246. Should you have a test for each code module?

247. The Knowledge Workers projected business base for each period?

248. Actual cost of work performed?

249. Is work progressively subdivided into detailed work packages as requirements are defined?

250. Are data elements summarized through the functional organizational structure for progressively higher levels of management?

251. Are estimates of costs at completion utilized in determining contract funding requirements and reporting them?

252. Are data being used by managers in an effective manner to ascertain Knowledge Workers project or functional status, to identify reasons or significant variance, and to initiate appropriate corrective action?

253. Intermediate schedules, as required, which provide a logical sequence from the master schedule to the control account level?

254. Are your organizations and items of cost assigned to each pool identified?

255. Are estimates of costs at completion generated in a rational, consistent manner?

256. Budgets assigned to major functional organizations?

257. Contractor financial periods; for example, annual?

2.10 Schedule Management Plan: Knowledge Workers

258. Will the Knowledge Workers project sponsor be involved in preliminary schedule reviews?

259. Are risk oriented checklists used during risk identification?

260. Are software metrics formally captured, analyzed and used as a basis for other Knowledge Workers project estimates?

261. Are all payments made according to the contract(s)?

262. Are metrics used to evaluate and manage Vendors?

263. Are mitigation strategies identified?

264. Are action items captured and managed?

265. Alignment to strategic goals & objectives?

266. Are adequate resources provided for the quality assurance function?

267. Are all key components of a Quality Assurance Plan present?

268. Are Knowledge Workers project contact logs kept up to date?

269. Was your organizations estimating methodology being used and followed?

270. Has process improvement efforts been completed before requirements efforts begin?

271. What weaknesses do you have?

272. Is an industry recognized mechanized support tool(s) being used for Knowledge Workers project scheduling & tracking?

273. Is quality monitored from the perspective of the customers needs and expectations?

274. Are the primary and secondary schedule tools defined?

275. Has the budget been baselined?

276. Have reserves been created to address risks?

277. Is current scope of the Knowledge Workers project substantially different than that originally defined?

2.11 Activity List: Knowledge Workers

278. Who will perform the work?

279. How can the Knowledge Workers project be displayed graphically to better visualize the activities?

280. How detailed should a Knowledge Workers project get?

281. How do you determine the late start (LS) for each activity?

282. What is the probability the Knowledge Workers project can be completed in xx weeks?

283. Can you determine the activity that must finish, before this activity can start?

284. The wbs is developed as part of a joint planning session. and how do you know that youhave done this right?

285. What did not go as well?

286. Is infrastructure setup part of your Knowledge Workers project?

287. How much slack is available in the Knowledge Workers project?

288. What are the critical bottleneck activities?

289. What is the total time required to complete the

Knowledge Workers project if no delays occur?

290. Should you include sub-activities?

291. What is the LF and LS for each activity?

292. How should ongoing costs be monitored to try to keep the Knowledge Workers project within budget?

293. What went right?

294. When will the work be performed?

295. What will be performed?

296. When do the individual activities need to start and finish?

2.12 Activity Attributes: Knowledge Workers

297. Does your organization of the data change its meaning?

298. Why?

299. Are the required resources available?

300. Can more resources be added?

301. How many resources do you need to complete the work scope within a limit of X number of days?

302. What is the general pattern here?

303. Have you identified the Activity Leveling Priority code value on each activity?

304. Activity: what is Missing?

305. Time for overtime?

306. Is there a trend during the year?

307. Has management defined a definite timeframe for the turnaround or Knowledge Workers project window?

308. How difficult will it be to do specific activities on this Knowledge Workers project?

309. Are the required resources available or need to be acquired?

310. How else could the items be grouped?

311. How many days do you need to complete the work scope with a limit of X number of resources?

312. What activity do you think you should spend the most time on?

313. Were there other ways you could have organized the data to achieve similar results?

314. What is your organizations history in doing similar activities?

2.13 Milestone List: Knowledge Workers

315. When will the Knowledge Workers project be complete?

316. What is the market for your technology, product or service?

317. Obstacles faced?

318. New USPs?

319. Gaps in capabilities?

320. Calculate how long can activity be delayed?

321. Marketing - reach, distribution, awareness?

322. Information and research?

323. How late can each activity be finished and started?

324. Sustaining internal capabilities?

325. Continuity, supply chain robustness?

326. Competitive advantages?

327. Legislative effects?

328. How difficult will it be to do specific activities on

this Knowledge Workers project?

329. Loss of key staff?

330. Political effects?

331. What are your competitors vulnerabilities?

332. What date will the task finish?

333. Do you foresee any technical risks or developmental challenges?

2.14 Network Diagram: Knowledge Workers

334. What is the lowest cost to complete this Knowledge Workers project in xx weeks?

335. What job or jobs follow it?

336. What is the probability of completing the Knowledge Workers project in less that xx days?

337. What controls the start and finish of a job?

338. What job or jobs could run concurrently?

339. What are the Major Administrative Issues?

340. What job or jobs precede it?

341. What activity must be completed immediately before this activity can start?

342. What must be completed before an activity can be started?

343. Where do you schedule uncertainty time?

344. What to do and When?

345. Why must you schedule milestones, such as reviews, throughout the Knowledge Workers project?

346. What activities must occur simultaneously with

this activity?

347. Which type of network diagram allows you to depict four types of dependencies?

348. What is the completion time?

349. What can be done concurrently?

350. What are the Key Success Factors?

351. Are you on time?

2.15 Activity Resource Requirements: Knowledge Workers

352. How many signatures do you require on a check and does this match what is in your policy and procedures?

353. Which logical relationship does the PDM use most often?

354. How do you handle petty cash?

355. Organizational Applicability?

356. What are constraints that you might find during the Human Resource Planning process?

357. Are there unresolved issues that need to be addressed?

358. Do you use tools like decomposition and rolling-wave planning to produce the activity list and other outputs?

359. When does monitoring begin?

360. Why do you do that?

361. Anything else?

362. What is the Work Plan Standard?

363. Is there anything planned that does not need to

be here?

364. Other support in specific areas?

2.16 Resource Breakdown Structure: Knowledge Workers

365. How can this help you with team building?

366. What defines a successful Knowledge Workers project?

367. Changes based on input from stakeholders?

368. The list could probably go on, but, the thing that you would most like to know is, How long & How much?

369. Is predictive resource analysis being done?

370. Who delivers the information?

371. Who is allowed to perform which functions?

372. What is the difference between % Complete and % work?

373. What is the number one predictor of a groups productivity?

374. Who needs what information?

375. What can you do to improve productivity?

376. Who is allowed to see what data about which resources?

377. What went wrong?

378. What is Knowledge Workers project communication management?

379. What is the purpose of assigning and documenting responsibility?

380. How should the information be delivered?

381. How difficult will it be to do specific activities on this Knowledge Workers project?

382. Why time management?

383. Who will use the system?

2.17 Activity Duration Estimates: Knowledge Workers

384. Is the work performed reviewed against contractual objectives?

385. What are two suggestions for ensuring adequate change control on Knowledge Workers projects that involve outside contracts?

386. What is wrong with this scenario?

387. Which type of mathematical analysis is being used?

388. Is a standard form used to obtain bids and proposals from prospective sellers?

389. Based on , if you need to shorten the duration of the Knowledge Workers project, what activity would you try to shorten?

390. How does poking fun at technical professionals communications skills impact the industry and educational programs?

391. What are the ways to create and distribute Knowledge Workers project performance information?

392. What is the critical path for this Knowledge Workers project and how long is it?

393. How does a Knowledge Workers project life cycle differ from a product life cycle?

394. Are actual Knowledge Workers project results compared with planned or expected results to determine the variance?

395. Why should Knowledge Workers project managers strive to make jobs look easy?

396. Do your results resemble a normal distribution?

397. Do procedures exist describing how the Knowledge Workers project scope will be managed?

398. It under budget or over budget?

399. What does it mean to take a systems view of a Knowledge Workers project?

400. Which is a benefit of an analogous Knowledge Workers project estimate?

2.18 Duration Estimating Worksheet: Knowledge Workers

401. Small or large Knowledge Workers project?

402. Why estimate costs?

403. What is the total time required to complete the Knowledge Workers project if no delays occur?

404. What is next?

405. Can the Knowledge Workers project be constructed as planned?

406. What is an Average Knowledge Workers project?

407. What is cost and Knowledge Workers project cost management?

408. When, then?

409. Is this operation cost effective?

410. What info is needed?

411. Why estimate time and cost?

412. Does the Knowledge Workers project provide innovative ways for stakeholders to overcome obstacles or deliver better outcomes?

413. Value pocket identification & quantification what

are value pockets?

414. Done before proceeding with this activity or what can be done concurrently?

415. What work will be included in the Knowledge Workers project?

416. Science = process: remember the scientific method?

417. Is a construction detail attached (to aid in explanation)?

418. How should ongoing costs be monitored to try to keep the Knowledge Workers project within budget?

419. What utility impacts are there?

2.19 Project Schedule: Knowledge Workers

420. Why is software Knowledge Workers project disaster so common?

421. What does that mean?

422. Master Knowledge Workers project schedule?

423. Are the original Knowledge Workers project schedule and budget realistic?

424. Is Knowledge Workers project work proceeding in accordance with the original Knowledge Workers project schedule?

425. How closely did the initial Knowledge Workers project Schedule compare with the actual schedule?

426. Is the structure for tracking the Knowledge Workers project schedule well defined and assigned to a specific individual?

427. Are you working on the right risks?

428. Did the Knowledge Workers project come in on schedule?

429. Your best shot for providing estimations how complex/how much work does the activity require?

430. How can slack be negative?

431. Are procedures defined by which the Knowledge Workers project schedule may be changed?

432. Activity charts and bar charts are graphical representations of a Knowledge Workers project schedule ...how do they differ?

433. Are quality inspections and review activities listed in the Knowledge Workers project schedule(s)?

434. How can you minimize or control changes to Knowledge Workers project schedules?

435. How detailed should a Knowledge Workers project get?

436. Did the final product meet or exceed user expectations?

437. Was the Knowledge Workers project schedule reviewed by all stakeholders and formally accepted?

438. Your Knowledge Workers project management plan results in a Knowledge Workers project schedule that is too long. If the Knowledge Workers project network diagram cannot change and you have extra personnel resources, what is the BEST thing to do?

439. If there are any qualifying green components to this Knowledge Workers project, what portion of the total Knowledge Workers project cost is green?

2.20 Cost Management Plan: Knowledge Workers

440. Cost variances – how will cost variances be identified and corrected?

441. How difficult will it be to do specific tasks on the Knowledge Workers project?

442. What are the nine areas of expertise?

443. Are vendor contract reports, reviews and visits conducted periodically?

444. Similar Knowledge Workers projects?

445. Are the schedule estimates reasonable given the Knowledge Workers project?

446. Schedule contingency – how will the schedule contingency be administrated?

447. Are cause and effect determined for risks when others occur?

448. Has a structured approach been used to break work effort into manageable components (WBS)?

449. Are there checklists created to determine if all quality processes are followed?

450. Contingency rundown curve be used on the Knowledge Workers project?

451. Are decisions captured in a decisions log?

452. Has the Knowledge Workers project scope been baselined?

453. Has the scope management document been updated and distributed to help prevent scope creep?

454. Are changes in scope (deliverable commitments) agreed to by all affected groups & individuals?

455. Have adequate resources been provided by management to ensure Knowledge Workers project success?

456. Have activity relationships and interdependencies within tasks been adequately identified?

457. Are changes in deliverable commitments agreed to by all affected groups & individuals?

458. Will the earned value reporting interface between time and cost management?

2.21 Activity Cost Estimates: Knowledge Workers

459. In which phase of the acquisition process cycle does source qualifications reside?

460. Certification of actual expenditures?

461. Where can you get activity reports?

462. Eac -estimate at completion, what is the total job expected to cost?

463. Were you satisfied with the work?

464. What were things that you need to improve?

465. What is a Knowledge Workers project Management Plan?

466. What is included in indirect cost being allocated?

467. What makes a good expected result statement?

468. Estimated cost?

469. Who determines the quality and expertise of contractors?

470. How do you fund change orders?

471. Why do you manage cost?

472. What makes a good activity description?

473. How do you allocate indirect costs to activities?

474. Scope statement only direct or indirect costs as well?

475. How many activities should you have?

476. What is the activity inventory?

477. What are the audit requirements?

478. The impact and what actions were taken?

2.22 Cost Estimating Worksheet: Knowledge Workers

479. Does the Knowledge Workers project provide innovative ways for stakeholders to overcome obstacles or deliver better outcomes?

480. Is it feasible to establish a control group arrangement?

481. What is the estimated labor cost today based upon this information?

482. Can a trend be established from historical performance data on the selected measure and are the criteria for using trend analysis or forecasting methods met?

483. Ask: are others positioned to know, are others credible, and will others cooperate?

484. How will the results be shared and to whom?

485. What costs are to be estimated?

486. Will the Knowledge Workers project collaborate with the local community and leverage resources?

487. Is the Knowledge Workers project responsive to community need?

488. What happens to any remaining funds not used?

489. Identify the timeframe necessary to monitor progress and collect data to determine how the selected measure has changed?

490. What will others want?

491. What is the purpose of estimating?

492. What additional Knowledge Workers project(s) could be initiated as a result of this Knowledge Workers project?

493. What can be included?

494. Who is best positioned to know and assist in identifying corresponding factors?

2.23 Cost Baseline: Knowledge Workers

495. Pcs for your new business. what would the life cycle costs be?

496. At which frequency ?

497. On time?

498. Has training and knowledge transfer of the operations organization been completed?

499. Has the Knowledge Workers project (or Knowledge Workers project phase) been evaluated against each objective established in the product description and Integrated Knowledge Workers project Plan?

500. What is cost and Knowledge Workers project cost management?

501. What threats might prevent you from getting there?

502. What is the consequence?

503. Has the appropriate access to relevant data and analysis capability been granted?

504. Have all the product or service deliverables been accepted by the customer?

505. How difficult will it be to do specific tasks on the Knowledge Workers project?

506. What deliverables come first?

507. Does the suggested change request represent a desired enhancement to the products functionality?

508. How likely is it to go wrong?

509. What can go wrong?

510. What is the most important thing to do next to make your Knowledge Workers project successful?

511. Has the actual cost of the Knowledge Workers project (or Knowledge Workers project phase) been tallied and compared to the approved budget?

512. What does a good WBS NOT look like?

2.24 Quality Management Plan: Knowledge Workers

513. How do you ensure that protocols are up to date?

514. Sampling part of task?

515. Would impacts defined serve as impediments?

516. Who is responsible?

517. How effectively was the Quality Management Plan applied during Knowledge Workers project Execution?

518. How do senior leaders review organizational performance?

519. How does your organization establish and maintain customer relationships?

520. How does your organization manage work to promote cooperation, individual initiative, innovation, flexibility, communications, and knowledge/skill sharing across work units?

521. How are corresponding standards measured?

522. How do you manage quality?

523. How does training support what is important to your organization and the individual?

524. What are your results for key measures/indicators of accomplishment of organizational strategy?

525. Is there a procedure for this process?

526. What are your organizations current levels and trends for the already stated measures related to customer satisfaction/ dissatisfaction and product/ service performance?

527. How does your organization recruit, hire, and retain new employees?

2.25 Quality Metrics: Knowledge Workers

528. Has it met internal or external standards?

529. Do the operators focus on determining; is there anything you need to worry about?

530. Which are the right metrics to use?

531. What if the biggest risk to your business were the already stated people who do not complain?

532. When is the security analysis testing complete?

533. Are interface issues coordinated?

534. Is there a set of procedures to capture, analyze and act on quality metrics?

535. What level of statistical confidence do you use?

536. Was review conducted per standard protocols?

537. Is quality culture a competitive advantage?

538. What are your organizations next steps?

539. Are there already quality metrics available that detect nonlinear embeddings and trends similar to the users perception?

540. Did the team meet the Knowledge Workers

project success criteria documented in the Quality Metrics Matrix?

541. What is the timeline to meet your goal?

542. What is the benchmark?

543. Are quality metrics defined?

544. What happens if you get an abnormal result?

545. What are your organizations expectations for its quality Knowledge Workers project?

2.26 Process Improvement Plan: Knowledge Workers

546. What actions are needed to address the problems and achieve the goals?

547. Are you making progress on the improvement framework?

548. Where do you want to be?

549. Why do you want to achieve the goal?

550. What is the return on investment?

551. Are you following the quality standards?

552. Modeling current processes is great, and will you ever see a return on that investment?

553. What makes people good SPI coaches?

554. What personnel are the change agents for your initiative?

555. Are there forms and procedures to collect and record the data?

556. Are you making progress on the goals?

557. What personnel are the champions for the initiative?

558. Has a process guide to collect the data been developed?

559. Are you meeting the quality standards?

560. The motive is determined by asking, Why do you want to achieve this goal?

561. What personnel are the sponsors for that initiative?

562. Purpose of goal: the motive is determined by asking, why do you want to achieve this goal?

563. What personnel are the coaches for your initiative?

2.27 Responsibility Assignment Matrix: Knowledge Workers

564. Does the contractors system identify work accomplishment against the schedule plan?

565. What simple tool can you use to help identify and prioritize Knowledge Workers project risks that is very low tech and high touch?

566. Does each role with Accountable responsibility have the authority within your organization to make the required decisions?

567. Are others working on the right things?

568. The total budget for the contract (including estimates for authorized and unpriced work)?

569. Are people afraid to let you know when others are under allocated?

570. Is the entire contract planned in time-phased control accounts to the extent practicable?

571. Are all authorized tasks assigned to identified organizational elements?

572. Are significant decision points, constraints, and interfaces identified as key milestones?

573. Too many is: do all the identified roles need to be routinely informed or only in exceptional

circumstances?

574. How do you manage human resources?

575. Is data disseminated to the contractors management timely, accurate, and usable?

576. What travel needed?

577. Is accountability placed at the lowest-possible level within the Knowledge Workers project so that decisions can be made at that level?

578. What tool can show you individual and group allocations?

579. Are records maintained to show how management reserves are used?

580. What cost control tool do many experts say is crucial to Knowledge Workers project management?

2.28 Roles and Responsibilities: Knowledge Workers

581. Authority: what areas/Knowledge Workers projects in your work do you have the authority to decide upon and act on the already stated decisions?

582. Concern: where are you limited or have no authority, where you can not influence?

583. Where are you most strong as a supervisor?

584. Does your vision/mission support a culture of quality data?

585. Influence: what areas of organizational decision making are you able to influence when you do not have authority to make the final decision?

586. Are governance roles and responsibilities documented?

587. Was the expectation clearly communicated?

588. Once the responsibilities are defined for the Knowledge Workers project, have the deliverables, roles and responsibilities been clearly communicated to every participant?

589. Is there a training program in place for stakeholders covering expectations, roles and responsibilities and any addition knowledge others need to be good stakeholders?

590. What is working well?

591. Is feedback clearly communicated and non-judgmental?

592. Are your policies supportive of a culture of quality data?

593. How is your work-life balance?

594. What expectations were NOT met?

595. What should you do now to ensure that you are exceeding expectations and excelling in your current position?

596. What should you highlight for improvement?

597. Have you ever been a part of this team?

598. What areas of supervision are challenging for you?

599. What should you do now to prepare yourself for a promotion, increased responsibilities or a different job?

600. What are your major roles and responsibilities in the area of performance measurement and assessment?

2.29 Human Resource Management Plan: Knowledge Workers

601. Are the quality tools and methods identified in the Quality Plan appropriate to the Knowledge Workers project?

602. Are there dependencies with other initiatives or Knowledge Workers projects?

603. Does the schedule include Knowledge Workers project management time and change request analysis time?

604. Is there a formal set of procedures supporting Issues Management?

605. Has a sponsor been identified?

606. Is there a set of procedures defining the scope, procedures, and deliverables defining quality control?

607. Who is evaluated?

608. Does the Knowledge Workers project have a Quality Culture?

609. Are milestone deliverables effectively tracked and compared to Knowledge Workers project plan?

610. Knowledge Workers project definition & scope?

611. Is the assigned Knowledge Workers project

manager a PMP (Certified Knowledge Workers project manager) and experienced?

612. Is Knowledge Workers project status reviewed with the steering and executive teams at appropriate intervals?

613. Is Knowledge Workers project work proceeding in accordance with the original Knowledge Workers project schedule?

614. How to convince to employees that it is a necessary process?

615. Are enough systems & user personnel assigned to the Knowledge Workers project?

616. Is the manpower level sufficient to meet the future business requirements?

2.30 Communications Management Plan: Knowledge Workers

617. Which stakeholders can influence others?

618. Conflict resolution -which method when?

619. Who to learn from?

620. What to learn?

621. Are others needed?

622. Are there potential barriers between the team and the stakeholder?

623. What approaches do you use?

624. Do you prepare stakeholder engagement plans?

625. What is Knowledge Workers project communications management?

626. Who did you turn to if you had questions?

627. How were corresponding initiatives successful?

628. Are stakeholders internal or external?

629. Why do you manage communications?

630. How much time does it take to do it?

631. Will messages be directly related to the release strategy or phases of the Knowledge Workers project?

632. Are there common objectives between the team and the stakeholder?

633. Where do team members get information?

634. Is the stakeholder role recognized by your organization?

635. Are the stakeholders getting the information others need, are others consulted, are concerns addressed?

636. What does the stakeholder need from the team?

2.31 Risk Management Plan: Knowledge Workers

637. Are the software tools integrated with each other?

638. Workarounds are determined during which step of risk management?

639. Are enough people available?

640. People risk -are people with appropriate skills available to help complete the Knowledge Workers project?

641. Are tool mentors available?

642. Is security a central objective?

643. What risks are necessary to achieve success?

644. Is the customer technically sophisticated in the product area?

645. Is there additional information that would make you more confident about your analysis?

646. Who has experience with this?

647. Are testing tools available and suitable?

648. Was an original risk assessment/risk management plan completed?

649. What will the damage be?

650. Is the process supported by tools?

651. Have customers been involved fully in the definition of requirements?

652. Can you stabilize dynamic risk factors?

653. Premium on reliability of product?

654. Technology risk: is the Knowledge Workers project technically feasible?

655. Have top software and customer managers formally committed to support the Knowledge Workers project?

2.32 Risk Register: Knowledge Workers

656. What should the audit role be in establishing a risk management process?

657. Are implemented controls working as others should?

658. Which key risks have ineffective responses or outstanding improvement actions?

659. How could corresponding Risk affect the Knowledge Workers project in terms of cost and schedule?

660. How often will the Risk Management Plan and Risk Register be formally reviewed, and by whom?

661. What would the impact to the Knowledge Workers project objectives be should the risk arise?

662. What is the reason for current performance gaps and do the risks and opportunities identified previously account for this?

663. Who is accountable?

664. Does the evidence highlight any areas to advance opportunities or foster good relations. If yes what steps will be taken?

665. What has changed since the last period?

666. What should you do when?

667. User involvement: do you have the right users?

668. How well are risks controlled?

669. What action, if any, has been taken to respond to the risk?

670. What is the probability and impact of the risk occurring?

671. Is further information required before making a decision?

672. Have other controls and solutions been implemented in other services which could be applied as an alternative to additional funding?

673. Are there any knock-on effects/impact on any of the other areas?

674. Who is going to do it?

2.33 Probability and Impact Assessment: Knowledge Workers

675. Do you have a mechanism for managing change?

676. My Knowledge Workers project leader has suddenly left your organization, what do you do?

677. How solid is the Knowledge Workers projection of competitive reaction?

678. What should be the gestation period for the Knowledge Workers project with specific technology?

679. What things are likely to change?

680. What are the current demands of the customer?

681. Will there be an increase in the political conservatism?

682. Is the number of people on the Knowledge Workers project team adequate to do the job?

683. Monitoring of the overall Knowledge Workers project status – are there any changes in the Knowledge Workers project that can effect and cause new possible risks?

684. Is the present organizational structure for handling the Knowledge Workers project sufficient?

685. Anticipated volatility of the requirements?

686. What is the probability of the risk occurring?

687. How are the local factors going to affect the absorption?

688. What are the chances the event will occur?

689. Should the risk be taken at all?

690. What are your data sources?

691. What would be the effect of slippage?

692. What will be the likely political environment during the life of the Knowledge Workers project?

2.34 Probability and Impact Matrix: Knowledge Workers

693. What are the current requirements of the customer?

694. How to prioritize risks?

695. Have you worked with the customer in the past?

696. What is your anticipated volatility of the requirements?

697. Costs associated with late delivery or a defective product?

698. Do end-users have realistic expectations?

699. Which role do you have in the Knowledge Workers project?

700. Why do you need to manage Knowledge Workers project Risk?

701. Do the people have the right combinations of skills?

702. Are some people working on multiple Knowledge Workers projects?

703. Have top software and customer managers formally committed to support the Knowledge Workers project?

704. Were there any Knowledge Workers projects similar to this one in existence?

705. What is the impact if the risk does occur?

706. How well were you able to manage your risk?

707. What are the methods to deal with risks?

708. What should be done with risks on the watch list?

709. My Knowledge Workers project leader has suddenly left your organization, what do you do?

710. Is the delay in one subKnowledge Workers project going to affect another?

711. What will be the environmental impact of the Knowledge Workers project?

712. Are tools for analysis and design available?

2.35 Risk Data Sheet: Knowledge Workers

713. Do effective diagnostic tests exist?

714. What is the chance that it will happen?

715. What if client refuses?

716. What are the main threats to your existence?

717. How reliable is the data source?

718. Potential for recurrence?

719. If it happens, what are the consequences?

720. Has a sensitivity analysis been carried out?

721. Risk of what?

722. What are you trying to achieve (Objectives)?

723. What will be the consequences if it happens?

724. What is the environment within which you operate (social trends, economic, community values, broad based participation, national directions etc.)?

725. How can hazards be reduced?

726. How can it happen?

727. Whom do you serve (customers)?

728. What is the likelihood of it happening?

729. What are you weak at and therefore need to do better?

730. What are you here for (Mission)?

731. What can happen?

2.36 Procurement Management Plan: Knowledge Workers

732. Has a capability assessment been conducted?

733. Have stakeholder accountabilities & responsibilities been clearly defined?

734. Were escalated issues resolved promptly?

735. Has a provision been made to reassess Knowledge Workers project risks at various Knowledge Workers project stages?

736. Are procurement deliverables arriving on time and to specification?

737. Are assumptions being identified, recorded, analyzed, qualified and closed?

738. Is the Knowledge Workers project sponsor clearly communicating the business case or rationale for why this Knowledge Workers project is needed?

739. Has a resource management plan been created?

740. Is there a procurement management plan in place?

741. How will multiple providers be managed?

742. Are key risk mitigation strategies added to the Knowledge Workers project schedule?

743. Are the Knowledge Workers project team members located locally to the users/stakeholders?

744. Are milestone deliverables effectively tracked and compared to Knowledge Workers project plan?

745. Has Knowledge Workers project success criteria been defined?

746. Do you have the reasons why the changes to your organizational systems and capabilities are required?

747. What areas are overlooked on this Knowledge Workers project?

748. Are status reports received per the Knowledge Workers project Plan?

2.37 Source Selection Criteria: Knowledge Workers

749. What should be considered when developing evaluation standards?

750. What information may not be provided?

751. Are there any specific considerations that precludes offers from being selected as the awardee?

752. How and when do you enter into Knowledge Workers project Procurement Management?

753. Do proposed hours support content and schedule?

754. How much past performance information should be requested?

755. What documentation is necessary regarding electronic communications?

756. How long will it take for the purchase cost to be the same as the lease cost?

757. How can the methods of publicizing the buy be tailored to yield more effective price competition?

758. Can you reasonably estimate total organization requirements for the coming year?

759. With the rapid changes in information

technology, will media be readable in five or ten years?

760. Are considerations anticipated?

761. How important is cost in the source selection decision relative to past performance and technical considerations?

762. How do you ensure an integrated assessment of proposals?

763. What source selection software is your team using?

764. Are evaluators ready to begin this task?

765. What management structure does your organization consider as optimal for performing the contract?

766. Who must be notified?

767. In order of importance, which evaluation criteria are the most critical to the determination of your overall rating?

768. When and what information can be considered with offerors regarding past performance?

2.38 Stakeholder Management Plan: Knowledge Workers

769. Are the key elements of a Knowledge Workers project Charter present?

770. Are the appropriate IT resources adequate to meet planned commitments?

771. How are you doing/what can be done better?

772. Are Knowledge Workers project contact logs kept up to date?

773. What proven methodologies and standards will be used to ensure that materials, products, processes and services are fit for purpose?

774. Does the system design reflect the requirements?

775. Are best practices and metrics employed to identify issues, progress, performance, etc.?

776. Are cause and effect determined for risks when they occur?

777. Is there any form of automated support for Issues Management?

778. Has the schedule been baselined?

779. What potential impact does the stakeholder have on the Knowledge Workers project?

780. Does the Knowledge Workers project have a Statement of Work?

781. Do all stakeholders know how to access this repository and where to find the Knowledge Workers project documentation?

782. Which of the records created within the Knowledge Workers project, if any, does the Business Owner require access to?

783. Is there an issues management plan in place?

784. Are formal code reviews conducted?

785. Are issues raised, assessed, actioned, and resolved in a timely and efficient manner?

2.39 Change Management Plan: Knowledge Workers

786. What work practices will be affected?

787. Is a training information sheet available?

788. What new roles are needed?

789. What did the people around you say about it?

790. Has the relevant business unit been notified of installation and support requirements?

791. What is the reason for the communication?

792. What is the most cynical response it can receive?

793. What prerequisite knowledge do corresponding groups need?

794. What are the training strategies?

795. When developing your communication plan do you address : When should the given message be communicated?

796. Will the culture embrace or reject this change?

797. Are there any restrictions on who can receive the communications?

798. Is there a software application relevant to this

deliverable?

799. What is the negative impact of communicating too soon or too late?

800. Has the priority for this Knowledge Workers project been set by the Business Unit Management Team?

801. What is the worst thing that can happen if you chose not to communicate this information?

802. What does a resilient organization look like?

803. What are the specific target groups / audience that will be impacted by this change?

804. What can you do to minimise misinterpretation and negative perceptions?

805. Do you need a new organization structure?

3.0 Executing Process Group: Knowledge Workers

806. Is the schedule for the set products being met?

807. What are the critical steps involved with strategy mapping?

808. What are the key components of the Knowledge Workers project communications plan?

809. Who are the Knowledge Workers project stakeholders?

810. Is the program supported by national and/or local organizations?

811. When do you share the scorecard with managers?

812. How could stakeholders negatively impact your Knowledge Workers project?

813. What is involved in the solicitation process?

814. What are some crucial elements of a good Knowledge Workers project plan?

815. When is the appropriate time to bring the scorecard to Board meetings?

816. Do Knowledge Workers project managers understand your organizational context for

Knowledge Workers projects?

817. What type of information goes in the quality assurance plan?

818. Were sponsors and decision makers available when needed outside regularly scheduled meetings?

819. On which process should team members spend the most time?

820. How will professionals learn what is expected from them what the deliverables are?

821. Will outside resources be needed to help?

822. Will a new application be developed using existing hardware, software, and networks?

823. What are crucial elements of successful Knowledge Workers project plan execution?

824. How well defined and documented were the Knowledge Workers project management processes you chose to use?

3.1 Team Member Status Report: Knowledge Workers

825. Are your organizations Knowledge Workers projects more successful over time?

826. Why is it to be done?

827. What specific interest groups do you have in place?

828. How does this product, good, or service meet the needs of the Knowledge Workers project and your organization as a whole?

829. Do you have an Enterprise Knowledge Workers project Management Office (EPMO)?

830. When a teams productivity and success depend on collaboration and the efficient flow of information, what generally fails them?

831. Is there evidence that staff is taking a more professional approach toward management of your organizations Knowledge Workers projects?

832. Are the products of your organizations Knowledge Workers projects meeting customers objectives?

833. Does every department have to have a Knowledge Workers project Manager on staff?

834. How it is to be done?

835. What is to be done?

836. How much risk is involved?

837. How can you make it practical?

838. Will the staff do training or is that done by a third party?

839. Does your organization have the means (staff, money, contract, etc.) to produce or to acquire the product, good, or service?

840. Does the product, good, or service already exist within your organization?

841. How will resource planning be done?

842. The problem with Reward & Recognition Programs is that the truly deserving people all too often get left out. How can you make it practical?

843. Are the attitudes of staff regarding Knowledge Workers project work improving?

3.2 Change Request: Knowledge Workers

844. How shall the implementation of changes be recorded?

845. How are changes graded and who is responsible for the rating?

846. What has an inspector to inspect and to check?

847. Who is included in the change control team?

848. How can changes be graded?

849. Have all related configuration items been properly updated?

850. Are you implementing itil processes?

851. What type of changes does change control take into account?

852. What can be filed?

853. Are there requirements attributes that are strongly related to the complexity and size?

854. Has a formal technical review been conducted to assess technical correctness?

855. Why control change across the life cycle?

856. Customer acceptance plan how will the customer verify the change has been implemented successfully?

857. What is the relationship between requirements attributes and reliability?

858. Will this change conflict with other requirements changes (e.g., lead to conflicting operational scenarios)?

859. Who can suggest changes?

860. How do team members communicate with each other?

861. What is the change request log?

862. Who will perform the change?

3.3 Change Log: Knowledge Workers

863. When was the request submitted?

864. Is the submitted change a new change or a modification of a previously approved change?

865. Is this a mandatory replacement?

866. Will the Knowledge Workers project fail if the change request is not executed?

867. Who initiated the change request?

868. Should a more thorough impact analysis be conducted?

869. How does this change affect the timeline of the schedule?

870. When was the request approved?

871. Is the change backward compatible without limitations?

872. How does this relate to the standards developed for specific business processes?

873. How does this change affect scope?

874. Is the change request within Knowledge Workers project scope?

875. Is the requested change request a result of

changes in other Knowledge Workers project(s)?

876. Is the change request open, closed or pending?

877. Do the described changes impact on the integrity or security of the system?

878. Does the suggested change request seem to represent a necessary enhancement to the product?

879. Where do changes come from?

3.4 Decision Log: Knowledge Workers

880. Who is the decisionmaker?

881. Who will be given a copy of this document and where will it be kept?

882. How does the use a Decision Support System influence the strategies/tactics or costs?

883. It becomes critical to track and periodically revisit both operational effectiveness; Are you noticing all that you need to, and are you interpreting what you see effectively?

884. Is everything working as expected?

885. What is the line where eDiscovery ends and document review begins?

886. What was the rationale for the decision?

887. Do strategies and tactics aimed at less than full control reduce the costs of management or simply shift the cost burden?

888. What makes you different or better than others companies selling the same thing?

889. Behaviors; what are guidelines that the team has identified that will assist them with getting the most out of team meetings?

890. What eDiscovery problem or issue did your

organization set out to fix or make better?

891. Which variables make a critical difference?

892. Linked to original objective?

893. Adversarial environment. is your opponent open to a non-traditional workflow, or will it likely challenge anything you do?

894. At what point in time does loss become unacceptable?

895. How do you define success?

896. What are the cost implications?

897. What is your overall strategy for quality control / quality assurance procedures?

898. How consolidated and comprehensive a story can you tell by capturing currently available incident data in a central location and through a log of key decisions during an incident?

899. How does provision of information, both in terms of content and presentation, influence acceptance of alternative strategies?

3.5 Quality Audit: Knowledge Workers

900. How does your organization know that it is maintaining a conducive staff climate?

901. Has a written procedure been established to identify devices during all stages of receipt, reconditioning, distribution and installation so that mix-ups are prevented?

902. How does your organization know that the range and quality of its accommodation, catering and transportation services are appropriately effective and constructive?

903. How does your organization ensure that equipment is appropriately maintained and producing valid results?

904. Is quality audit a prerequisite for program accreditation or program recognition?

905. Does the audit organization have experience in performing the required work for entities of your type and size?

906. How does your organization know that its system for inducting new staff to maximize workplace contributions are appropriately effective and constructive?

907. Does the report read coherently?

908. How does your organization know that its

financial management system is appropriately effective and constructive?

909. How does your organization know that its systems for assisting staff with career planning and employment placements are appropriately effective and constructive?

910. How does the organization know that its system for maintaining and advancing the capabilities of its staff, particularly in relation to the Mission of the organization, is appropriately effective and constructive?

911. How does your organization know that the review processes are effective?

912. Are measuring and test equipment that have been placed out of service suitably identified and excluded from use in any device reconditioning operation?

913. How are you auditing your organizations compliance with regulations?

914. How do staff know if they are doing a good job?

915. Is your organizational structure established and each positions responsibility defined?

916. How does your organization know that its advisory services are appropriately effective and constructive?

917. How does your organization know that the system for managing its facilities is appropriately

effective and constructive?

918. What are your supplier audits?

919. Are training programs documented?

3.6 Team Directory: Knowledge Workers

920. What are you going to deliver or accomplish?

921. What needs to be communicated?

922. Have you decided when to celebrate the Knowledge Workers projects completion date?

923. Who are your stakeholders (customers, sponsors, end users, team members)?

924. How and in what format should information be presented?

925. Contract requirements complied with?

926. Where will the product be used and/or delivered or built when appropriate?

927. Process decisions: are all start-up, turn over and close out requirements of the contract satisfied?

928. Who will write the meeting minutes and distribute?

929. Days from the time the issue is identified?

930. Who will report Knowledge Workers project status to all stakeholders?

931. Process decisions: do invoice amounts match

accepted work in place?

932. Is construction on schedule?

933. Who are the Team Members?

934. Process decisions: are contractors adequately prosecuting the work?

935. How will you accomplish and manage the objectives?

936. Process decisions: do job conditions warrant additional actions to collect job information and document on-site activity?

937. How does the team resolve conflicts and ensure tasks are completed?

938. Process decisions: are there any statutory or regulatory issues relevant to the timely execution of work?

939. Who will talk to the customer?

3.7 Team Operating Agreement: Knowledge Workers

940. What administrative supports will be put in place to support the team and the teams supervisor?

941. Do team members need to frequently communicate as a full group to make timely decisions?

942. What resources can be provided for the team in terms of equipment, space, time for training, protected time and space for meetings, and travel allowances?

943. Do you prevent individuals from dominating the meeting?

944. Did you recap the meeting purpose, time, and expectations?

945. Why does your organization want to participate in teaming?

946. How will group handle unplanned absences?

947. Must your team members rely on the expertise of other members to complete tasks?

948. Confidentiality: how will confidential information be handled?

949. Are there more than two functional areas

represented by your team?

950. The method to be used in the decision making process; Will it be consensus, majority rule, or the supervisor having the final say?

951. Are there differences in access to communication and collaboration technology based on team member location?

952. What are the safety issues/risks that need to be addressed and/or that the team needs to consider?

953. How will you divide work equitably?

954. Resource allocation: how will individual team members account for time and expenses, and how will this be allocated in the team budget?

955. How will you resolve conflict efficiently and respectfully?

956. What are the current caseload numbers in the unit?

957. How does teaming fit in with overall organizational goals and meet organizational needs?

958. What is the anticipated procedure (recruitment, solicitation of volunteers, or assignment) for selecting team members?

959. What are some potential sources of conflict among team members?

3.8 Team Performance Assessment: Knowledge Workers

960. To what degree do team members frequently explore the teams purpose and its implications?

961. To what degree can the team ensure that all members are individually and jointly accountable for the teams purpose, goals, approach, and work-products?

962. To what degree will the team ensure that all members equitably share the work essential to the success of the team?

963. Delaying market entry: how long is too long?

964. To what degree do members understand and articulate the same purpose without relying on ambiguous abstractions?

965. How much interpersonal friction is there in your team?

966. How hard did you try to make a good selection?

967. To what degree do members articulate the goals beyond the team membership?

968. Is there a particular method of data analysis that you would recommend as a means of demonstrating that method variance is not of great concern for a given dataset?

969. Individual task proficiency and team process behavior: what is important for team functioning?

970. To what degree are the skill areas critical to team performance present?

971. To what degree are staff involved as partners in the improvement process?

972. To what degree will team members, individually and collectively, commit time to help themselves and others learn and develop skills?

973. To what degree will the approach capitalize on and enhance the skills of all team members in a manner that takes into consideration other demands on members of the team?

974. To what degree are corresponding categories of skills either actually or potentially represented across the membership?

975. What structural changes have you made or are you preparing to make?

976. Effects of crew composition on crew performance: Does the whole equal the sum of its parts?

977. To what degree does the team possess adequate membership to achieve its ends?

978. To what degree do the goals specify concrete team work products?

979. To what degree does the teams approach to its work allow for modification and improvement over time?

3.9 Team Member Performance Assessment: Knowledge Workers

980. How do you determine which data are the most important to use, analyze, or review?

981. Should a ratee get a copy of all the raters documents about the employees performance?

982. What stakeholders must be involved in the development and oversight of the performance plan?

983. What happens if a team member receives a Rating of Unsatisfactory?

984. To what extent did the evaluation influence the instructional path, such as with adaptive testing?

985. To what degree will new and supplemental skills be introduced as the need is recognized?

986. Do the goals support your organizations goals?

987. What are the basic principles and objectives of performance measurement and assessment?

988. How are evaluation results utilized?

989. What entity leads the process, selects a potential restructuring option and develops the plan?

990. Why were corresponding selected?

991. Does the rater (supervisor) have to wait for the interim or final performance assessment review to tell an employee that the employees performance is unsatisfactory?

992. For what period of time is a member rated?

993. Are there any safeguards to prevent intentional or unintentional rating errors?

994. What is needed for effective data teams?

995. How is the timing of assessments organized (e.g., pre/post-test, single point during training, multiple reassessment during training)?

996. What is the role of the Reviewer?

997. Are the goals SMART ?

998. How should adaptive assessments be implemented?

3.10 Issue Log: Knowledge Workers

999. What approaches to you feel are the best ones to use?

1000. Who reported the issue?

1001. Which stakeholders are thought leaders, influences, or early adopters?

1002. What date was the issue resolved?

1003. How do you manage communications?

1004. Who were proponents/opponents?

1005. Is there an important stakeholder who is actively opposed and will not receive messages?

1006. Persistence; will users learn a work around or will they be bothered every time?

1007. Is the issue log kept in a safe place?

1008. What is the impact on the Business Case?

1009. How often do you engage with stakeholders?

1010. What are the typical contents?

1011. Why do you manage human resources?

1012. Is access to the Issue Log controlled?

4.0 Monitoring and Controlling Process Group: Knowledge Workers

1013. How is agile program management done?

1014. What resources (both financial and non-financial) are available/needed?

1015. Just how important is your work to the overall success of the Knowledge Workers project?

1016. Are the services being delivered?

1017. Is there undesirable impact on staff or resources?

1018. Where is the Risk in the Knowledge Workers project?

1019. Do the partners have sufficient financial capacity to keep up the benefits produced by the programme?

1020. Is progress on outcomes due to your program?

1021. Is the program in place as intended?

1022. Did the Knowledge Workers project team have enough people to execute the Knowledge Workers project plan?

1023. What will you do to minimize the impact should a risk event occur?

1024. How was the program set-up initiated?

1025. Are there areas that need improvement?

1026. How many more potential communications channels were introduced by the discovery of the new stakeholders?

1027. How do you monitor progress?

1028. Did it work?

4.1 Project Performance Report: Knowledge Workers

1029. To what degree are the goals ambitious?

1030. To what degree can team members frequently and easily communicate with one another?

1031. To what degree does the teams work approach provide opportunity for members to engage in open interaction?

1032. To what degree does the informal organization make use of individual resources and meet individual needs?

1033. To what degree do all members feel responsible for all agreed-upon measures?

1034. To what degree does the information network provide individuals with the information they require?

1035. To what degree is the team cognizant of small wins to be celebrated along the way?

1036. To what degree does the teams purpose contain themes that are particularly meaningful and memorable?

1037. To what degree is there a sense that only the team can succeed?

1038. What is the PRS?

1039. To what degree do the structures of the formal organization motivate taskrelevant behavior and facilitate task completion?

1040. What degree are the relative importance and priority of the goals clear to all team members?

1041. To what degree are the tasks requirements reflected in the flow and storage of information?

1042. What is in it for you?

1043. How will procurement be coordinated with other Knowledge Workers project aspects, such as scheduling and performance reporting?

4.2 Variance Analysis: Knowledge Workers

1044. Are the overhead pools formally and adequately identified?

1045. Is all contract work included in the CWBS?

1046. What is the expected future profitability of each customer?

1047. What business event causes fluctuations?

1048. The anticipated business volume?

1049. What is the total budget for the Knowledge Workers project (including estimates for authorized and unpriced work)?

1050. Are procedures for variance analysis documented and consistently applied at the control account level and selected WBS and organizational levels at least monthly as a routine task?

1051. Favorable or unfavorable variance?

1052. Are all elements of indirect expense identified to overhead cost budgets of Knowledge Workers projections?

1053. How do you evaluate the impact of schedule changes, work around, et?

1054. Are there changes in the overhead pool and/or organization structures?

1055. Who is generally responsible for monitoring and taking action on variances?

1056. Are there quarterly budgets with quarterly performance comparisons?

1057. Does the accounting system provide a basis for auditing records of direct costs chargeable to the contract?

1058. Can process improvements lead to unfavorable variances?

1059. How are variances affected by multiple material and labor categories?

1060. What costs are avoidable if one or more customers are dropped?

1061. When, during the last four quarters, did a primary business event occur causing a fluctuation?

4.3 Earned Value Status: Knowledge Workers

1062. How much is it going to cost by the finish?

1063. When is it going to finish?

1064. What is the unit of forecast value?

1065. Where are your problem areas?

1066. Where is evidence-based earned value in your organization reported?

1067. Earned value can be used in almost any Knowledge Workers project situation and in almost any Knowledge Workers project environment. it may be used on large Knowledge Workers projects, medium sized Knowledge Workers projects, tiny Knowledge Workers projects (in cut-down form), complex and simple Knowledge Workers projects and in any market sector. some people, of course, know all about earned value, they have used it for years - but perhaps not as effectively as they could have?

1068. How does this compare with other Knowledge Workers projects?

1069. Verification is a process of ensuring that the developed system satisfies the stakeholders agreements and specifications; Are you building the product right? What do you verify?

1070. Validation is a process of ensuring that the developed system will actually achieve the stakeholders desired outcomes; Are you building the right product? What do you validate?

1071. Are you hitting your Knowledge Workers projects targets?

1072. If earned value management (EVM) is so good in determining the true status of a Knowledge Workers project and Knowledge Workers project its completion, why is it that hardly any one uses it in information systems related Knowledge Workers projects?

4.4 Risk Audit: Knowledge Workers

1073. Has risk management been considered when planning an event?

1074. Do you have a clear plan for the future that describes what you want to do and how you are going to do it?

1075. Are staff committed for the duration of the product?

1076. Are procedures in place to ensure the security of staff and information and compliance with privacy legislation if applicable?

1077. Are you aware of the industry standards that apply to your operations?

1078. Are audit program plans risk-adjusted?

1079. What are the differences and similarities between strategic and operational risks in your organization?

1080. Is the customer willing to participate in reviews?

1081. Can analytical tests provide evidence that is as strong as evidence from traditional substantive tests?

1082. The halo effect in business risk audits: can strategic risk assessment bias auditor judgment about accounting details?

1083. Do you have a procedure for dealing with complaints?

1084. What is happening in other jurisdictions? Could that happen here?

1085. Is the auditor able to evaluate contradictory evidence in an unbiased manner?

1086. What are the risks that could stop you from achieving your KPIs?

1087. Does the implementation method matter?

1088. Have risks been considered with an insurance broker or provider and suitable insurance cover been arranged?

1089. Do you have position descriptions for all key paid and volunteer positions in your organization?

1090. What is the Board doing to assure measurement and improve outcomes and quality and reduce avoidable adverse events?

1091. Do requirements put excessive performance constraints on the product?

1092. Are the best people available?

4.5 Contractor Status Report: Knowledge Workers

1093. What was the actual budget or estimated cost for your organizations services?

1094. If applicable; describe your standard schedule for new software version releases. Are new software version releases included in the standard maintenance plan?

1095. How does the proposed individual meet each requirement?

1096. Describe how often regular updates are made to the proposed solution. Are corresponding regular updates included in the standard maintenance plan?

1097. How is risk transferred?

1098. What was the final actual cost?

1099. What are the minimum and optimal bandwidth requirements for the proposed solution?

1100. Who can list a Knowledge Workers project as organization experience, your organization or a previous employee of your organization?

1101. Are there contractual transfer concerns?

1102. What process manages the contracts?

1103. What was the budget or estimated cost for your organizations services?

1104. How long have you been using the services?

1105. What was the overall budget or estimated cost?

1106. What is the average response time for answering a support call?

4.6 Formal Acceptance: Knowledge Workers

1107. Do you buy-in installation services?

1108. Does it do what client said it would?

1109. What is the Acceptance Management Process?

1110. Did the Knowledge Workers project manager and team act in a professional and ethical manner?

1111. What are the requirements against which to test, Who will execute?

1112. What function(s) does it fill or meet?

1113. What can you do better next time?

1114. Was the Knowledge Workers project goal achieved?

1115. Who would use it?

1116. Did the Knowledge Workers project achieve its MOV?

1117. How does your team plan to obtain formal acceptance on your Knowledge Workers project?

1118. Is formal acceptance of the Knowledge Workers project product documented and distributed?

1119. How well did the team follow the methodology?

1120. What lessons were learned about your Knowledge Workers project management methodology?

1121. Have all comments been addressed?

1122. Do you buy pre-configured systems or build your own configuration?

1123. General estimate of the costs and times to complete the Knowledge Workers project?

1124. Was the sponsor/customer satisfied?

1125. Do you perform formal acceptance or burn-in tests?

1126. Who supplies data?

5.0 Closing Process Group: Knowledge Workers

1127. How will staff learn how to use the deliverables?

1128. What is the Knowledge Workers project name and date of completion?

1129. What level of risk does the proposed budget represent to the Knowledge Workers project?

1130. What is the amount of funding and what Knowledge Workers project phases are funded?

1131. Were cost budgets met?

1132. What went well?

1133. How well did the chosen processes produce the expected results?

1134. What could be done to improve the process?

1135. Will the Knowledge Workers project deliverable(s) replace a current asset or group of assets?

1136. Were decisions made in a timely manner?

1137. Is the Knowledge Workers project funded?

1138. Can the lesson learned be replicated?

1139. Does the close educate others to improve performance?

1140. What were things that you did very well and want to do the same again on the next Knowledge Workers project?

1141. Did the Knowledge Workers project team have the right skills?

1142. Did you do what you said you were going to do?

1143. How dependent is the Knowledge Workers project on other Knowledge Workers projects or work efforts?

1144. Is this a follow-on to a previous Knowledge Workers project?

1145. What communication items need improvement?

5.1 Procurement Audit: Knowledge Workers

1146. Is the departments procurement function/unit well organized?

1147. Is the purchasing department organizationally independent of the departments using that function?

1148. Are signature plates under the control of someone other than the individual given check-signing accountability?

1149. Is there no evidence of any external or superior pressure to reach a specific result?

1150. Did your organization identify the full contract value and include options and provisions for renewals?

1151. Are procedures established so that vendors with poor quality or late delivery are identified to eliminate additional dealings with that vendor?

1152. Where applicable, did your organization adequately manage experts employed to assist in the procurement process?

1153. Was a formal review of tenders received undertaken?

1154. In case of time and material and labour hour contracts, does surveillance give an adequate and reasonable assurance that the contractor is using efficient methods and effective cost controls?

1155. Are all purchase orders signed by the purchasing agent?

1156. Is an appropriated degree of standardization of goods and services respected?

1157. Are trial balances taken weekly for general ledgers for all funds?

1158. Is the performance of the procurement function/unit benchmarked with other procurement functions/units in the different stages of the procurement process?

1159. Are the official minutes written in a clear and concise manner?

1160. Are criteria and sub-criteria set suitable to identify the tender that offers best value for money?

1161. Are there reasonable procedures to identify possible sources of supply?

1162. Are open purchase orders with a fixed monetary limitation used for local purchases of small dollar value?

1163. Does the contract include performance-based clauses?

1164. Have guidelines incorporating the principles and objectives of a robust procurement practice been established?

1165. When you set social or environmental conditions for the performance of the contract, were corresponding compatible with the law and was adequate information given to the candidates?

5.2 Contract Close-Out: Knowledge Workers

1166. Has each contract been audited to verify acceptance and delivery?

1167. Have all contracts been completed?

1168. How does it work?

1169. What is capture management?

1170. Why Outsource?

1171. Parties: Authorized?

1172. Was the contract sufficiently clear so as not to result in numerous disputes and misunderstandings?

1173. Have all contracts been closed?

1174. How/when used ?

1175. How is the contracting office notified of the automatic contract close-out?

1176. Are the signers the authorized officials?

1177. Was the contract type appropriate?

1178. Change in knowledge?

1179. Parties: who is involved?

1180. Have all contract records been included in the Knowledge Workers project archives?

1181. Was the contract complete without requiring numerous changes and revisions?

1182. What happens to the recipient of services?

1183. Have all acceptance criteria been met prior to final payment to contractors?

1184. Change in attitude or behavior?

1185. Change in circumstances?

5.3 Project or Phase Close-Out: Knowledge Workers

1186. Who exerted influence that has positively affected or negatively impacted the Knowledge Workers project?

1187. Is the lesson based on actual Knowledge Workers project experience rather than on independent research?

1188. What are the mandatory communication needs for each stakeholder?

1189. Does the lesson educate others to improve performance?

1190. What process was planned for managing issues/risks?

1191. What were the desired outcomes?

1192. In preparing the Lessons Learned report, should it reflect a consensus viewpoint, or should the report reflect the different individual viewpoints?

1193. What could have been improved?

1194. Did the delivered product meet the specified requirements and goals of the Knowledge Workers project?

1195. Planned completion date?

1196. In addition to assessing whether the Knowledge Workers project was successful, it is equally critical to analyze why it was or was not fully successful. Are you including this?

1197. Were the outcomes different from the already stated planned?

1198. What information is each stakeholder group interested in?

1199. When and how were information needs best met?

1200. What was the preferred delivery mechanism?

1201. What can you do better next time, and what specific actions can you take to improve?

1202. What information did each stakeholder need to contribute to the Knowledge Workers projects success?

1203. Were messages directly related to the release strategy or phases of the Knowledge Workers project?

1204. What is this stakeholder expecting?

5.4 Lessons Learned: Knowledge Workers

1205. How timely were Progress Reports provided to the Knowledge Workers project Manager by Team Members?

1206. How effective was the documentation that you received with the Knowledge Workers project product/service?

1207. What needs to be done over or differently?

1208. How effective were Best Practices & Lessons Learned from prior Knowledge Workers projects utilized in this Knowledge Workers project?

1209. How much communication is task-related?

1210. Where could you improve?

1211. What are the needs of the individuals?

1212. What were the key issues?

1213. What regulatory constraints impact the case?

1214. What rewards do the individuals seek?

1215. What would you change?

1216. What is your organizational ideology?

1217. How smooth do you feel Integration has been?

1218. Is there a clear cause and effect between the activity and the lesson learned?

1219. Were the Knowledge Workers project objectives met (if not, briefly account for what wasnt met)?

1220. How accurately and timely was the Risk Management Log updated or reviewed?

1221. How well prepared were you to receive Knowledge Workers project deliverables?

1222. Who had fiscal authority to manage the funding for the Knowledge Workers project, did that work?

1223. Where do you go from here?

1224. How does the budget cycle affect the case?

Index

267

educate   252, 258
education   26, 94
effect 137, 174, 200-201, 210, 245, 261
effective   16, 22, 114-115, 141, 148, 152, 170, 204, 208, 224-226, 235, 254, 260
effects 47, 130, 132, 160-161, 199, 232
efficiency   66, 92
efficient   56, 76, 211, 216, 254
effort   38, 44, 50, 57, 107, 135, 139, 174
efforts 31, 88, 131, 147, 155, 252
either 232
electronic   1, 208
elements   9, 34, 71, 96, 120, 151-152, 188, 210, 214-215, 241
eliminate   253
eliminated   147
embarking   32
embeddings 184
embrace   212
emergent   52
emerging   60, 100
employed   210, 253
employee   85, 117, 235, 247
employees   20, 22, 58, 109, 113, 115, 183, 193, 234-235
employers   129
employment 225
empower   7, 72
enable 68
enablers   108
encourage   87, 100
end-users   202
engage   117, 236, 239
engagement 47, 129, 194
enhance   94, 232
enhanced   117
enhancing   92
enough   7, 59, 112, 114, 140, 142, 193, 196, 237
ensure 33, 40, 69-70, 84, 111, 115, 117-119, 147-148, 175, 182, 191, 209-210, 224, 228, 231, 245
ensures   118
ensuring   9, 121, 168, 243-244
entail   44
Enterprise   216
entire 188

288

project 2-8, 16, 20, 22, 24-25, 41, 54, 63-65, 69, 77, 91, 98, 104-
107, 112, 118-120, 122, 124-127, 129-139, 142, 144-145, 147-149,
152, 154-158, 160-162, 166-176, 178-182, 185, 188-190, 192-198,
200-203, 206-208, 210-211, 213-217, 220-221, 227, 237, 239-241,
243-244, 247, 249-252, 257-261
projected   152
projection   200
projects   2, 50, 121, 124-125, 135, 142, 149, 168, 174, 190,
192, 202-203, 215-216, 227, 243-244, 252, 259-260
promising   122
promote   52, 182
promotion   191
promotions   137
promptly   206
proofing   86
proper 138
properly   34, 38, 151, 218
proponents   236
proposals   97, 168, 209
proposed   18, 49, 54, 131, 135, 208, 247, 251
protect   69, 109
protected   62, 229
protection   122
protocols   182, 184
proven 210
provide   23, 60, 115, 118, 122, 129, 152, 170, 178, 239, 242,
245
provided   11, 98, 137, 147, 154, 175, 208, 229, 260
provider   246
providers   84, 206
providing   129, 172
provision   206, 223
provisions   253
publisher   1
purchase   7, 208, 254
purchases   254
purchasing   253-254
purpose   2, 9, 120, 125, 127, 144, 167, 179, 187, 210, 229,
231, 239
purposes   135
pushing   112
qualified   34, 61, 65, 71, 134, 206
qualifies   60, 63

CPSIA information can be obtained
at www.ICGtesting.com
Printed in the USA
BVHW082019110819
555624BV00016BA/1838/P